HUGO LLORIS
EARNING MY SPURS

HUGO LLORIS
EARNING MY SPURS

A LIFE IN FOOTBALL FROM NICE TO LA AND BEYOND

In collaboration with Vincent Duluc

Translated by Roland Glasser

QUERCUS

First published in France in 2024 by Éditions Stock

First published in Great Britain in 2024 by

QUERCUS

Quercus Editions Limited
Carmelite House
50 Victoria Embankment
London EC4Y 0DZ

An Hachette UK company

The authorised representative in the EEA is Hachette Ireland,
8 Castlecourt Centre, Castleknock Road, Castleknock,
Dublin 15, D15 YF6A, Ireland

Copyright © 2024 Éditions Stock

The moral right of Hugo Lloris to be
identified as the author of this work has been
asserted in accordance with the Copyright,
Designs and Patents Act, 1988.

Translation Copyright © 2024 Roland Glasser

All rights reserved. No part of this publication
may be reproduced or transmitted in any form
or by any means, electronic or mechanical,
including photocopy, recording, or any
information storage and retrieval system,
without permission in writing from the publisher.

A CIP catalogue record for this book is available
from the British Library

HB ISBN 978 1 52944 288 5
TPB ISBN 978 1 52944 289 2
EBOOK ISBN 978 1 52944 290 8

Picture credits (in order of appearance):
1, 2, 3, 4, 5, 6, 7, 11 – courtesy of the author;
8 – © Pierre Lahalle/L'Équipe/Presse Sports;
9 – © Charlotte Wilson/OFFSIDE/Presse Sports; 10 – © Mao/L'Équipe/Presse Sports;
12 – © Christophe de Prada/Presse Sports; 13 – © Alexis Réau/L'Équipe/Presse Sports;
14 – © Franck Faugère/Presse Sports; 15 – © Pierre Lahalle/ L'Équipe/Presse Sports;
16 – © Pierre Lahalle/ L'Équipe/Presse Sports

Quercus Editions Ltd hereby exclude all liability to the extent permitted by law for any errors or omissions in this book and for any loss, damage or expense (whether direct or indirect) suffered by a third party relying on any information contained in this book.

Typeset in Rotis Serif by CC Book Production
Printed and bound in Great Britain by Clays Ltd, Elcograf S.p.A.

MIX
Paper | Supporting
responsible forestry
FSC® C104740

Papers used by Quercus are from well-managed forests and other responsible sources.

Contents

I	Final Night	1
II	Decision Time	9
III	The Void	21
IV	'I Think I Want to Quit, Dad'	33
V	'Go For it, it's All Yours!'	51
VI	A Star in the Sky Over Nice	65
VII	Final Four	75
VIII	A Proper Playoff	89
IX	Knysna	99
X	A Cup	119
XI	Captain	129
XII	Hugo Who?	137
XIII	Brazil!	147
XIV	A Season in Hell	161

XV	Slightly Mad	175
XVI	The Pochettino Years	185
XVII	All the Gold in the World	203
XVIII	A Lesson	223
XIX	The Special One	233
XX	*Au Revoir Les Bleus!*	251
XXI	Life After	273
	Index	283
	Translator's Thanks	293

1

Final Night

I remember the pain. It's still there. And it won't let me forget. I can picture myself in the dressing room at Lusail Stadium, near Doha, seeking solitude amid everyone's sadness. To lose a World Cup final is the greatest defeat in a footballer's life. It shrouds the losers in mournful quiet. Four years earlier, in Moscow, I was in the other dressing room, the world champions' one: a sea of singing and celebration. But the night of 18 December 2022, a week before Christmas and eight days before my 36th birthday – where there'd be plenty of candles but one missing star – this defeat by Argentina bit deep. I felt awful, as if I'd been skewered, so bad in fact that I knew straight off that this wound would take a long time to heal, if it ever did, and that the scars would remain. When the animated clatter of studs on the dressing-room floor had ceased, we all began changing out of our kit in this heavy silence, though we'd long since

FINAL NIGHT

shed our armour, naked in the face of loss. Eventually I stood up and headed into the passageway to the showers in an attempt to hide myself from the world and the tears. Perhaps I was looking for another kind of silence.

Whenever I'm asked at what point this defeat in the final of the World Cup hurt me the most, I don't know what to reply: there wasn't a specific moment; it lasted three days at first, and for a long time after. The pain gradually slunk away into the fog of the following days, as if it had made a cocoon for itself, but it was never far away. If only you could lose a World Cup final without realizing what you've lost, without knowing that unbridgeable chasm between winners and losers, between their glory and your regret. It is painful to lose – it is even more painful to lose an action-packed final after so much hope – but to lose a World Cup final, in front of everyone you love, the pain of that is simply indescribable. My wife Marine and the children had been there from the second match; my father, his partner Ester and my grandmother had joined them for the round of 16. Now that it was all over, each of them truly realized that this had been the voyage of a lifetime, an exceptional immersion in our – in my – world throughout this World Cup. They remember it as some paradise lost. As for my mother and grandfather, who are no longer with us, I think about them before each match.

After the final penalty in the shootout against Argentina, I felt totally empty. I didn't want to be there, on that pitch of broken dreams where we'd fought to the last ounce of our strength. I was wiped out by this emotional rollercoaster, by this boxing match, one punch following the next, no let-up for a moment, no time to calculate, and that feeling of walking a tightrope the whole night, and then suddenly falling off it.

The pain of defeat is magnified for a goalkeeper following a penalty shootout. I looked for my family in the stands and saw they were as sad as I was. My brother Gautier, who plays in Ligue 1 for Le Havre, had arrived at the last moment with Clémence, his girlfriend; we don't see enough of each other and would have hoped for a different outcome. The final was historic, but not in the way I'd have wished. Later, I'd meet people in the street who'd thank me for the beauty and emotional intensity of this final, assuring me that it was the most wonderful match they'd experienced in all their lives. Maybe when I'm old I'll be able to see it like that. But not yet: it was a disaster because we lost, because we were crap for 80 minutes. And so the pain was unbearable.

In the dressing room straight afterwards, the old guard and the injured who'd come to cheer us on, players such as Blaise Matuidi and N'Golo Kanté, tried to console us, but

FINAL NIGHT

they knew it was impossible. The deathly silence was broken only by a bustle at the door as President Macron appeared. He gave a moving speech, but it could do nothing for us right then, because we were inconsolable. When he'd finished talking, I went and found that place near the showers, as if I could rip myself away from the disappointment and leave it there in the dressing room.

Olivier Giroud and Raphaël Varane joined me, followed by our manager, Didier Deschamps. None of us said very much. Didier sighed: 'I'd have preferred to lose 3–0, and be done with it . . .' Actually, no, he wouldn't have, and neither would we. But when you come back from so far behind, from 0–2 to 2–2 in two minutes at the end of the match, then from 2–3 to 3–3 in extra time, you tell yourself you're going to do it, this incredible thing, despite having messed everything up for so long. It's always hope that does the most damage; and after 80 minutes it returned, and it was huge. It was because we got so close to the unimaginable, before falling away, then drew so close again, that the disappointment overwhelmed us. There's never been a World Cup final like it.

After my shower, I had to speak to the media: I was captain, after all, and this was World Cup final night. I said what I still think: that it hurt, but that we could be proud.

I got back on the bus and sat in my usual seat, to the

right of the middle door. All I wanted to do was go home. We gathered for dinner back at the hotel, but I had no appetite, I wasn't really there. It's not that I cold-shouldered anyone, I was just in my own world. I went up to bed knowing that I wouldn't sleep. Luckily I discovered a few years ago that the morning after an extraordinary day like a World Cup final, your children drag you back to reality: you've got to be there for them as soon as they wake, for breakfast. The flight home was almost pleasant because my three-year-old son fell asleep on me, his infant snoozing soothing my transition from this collective odyssey back to real life. It was a mellowness to ease all torments.

After landing in Paris on the Monday, we went straight to the balcony of the Hôtel de Crillon overlooking the Place de la Concorde, where the warm appreciation of thousands of fans did us a world of good. It was a reminder that we had gone on an epic adventure together. And for those few hours, the disappointment wasn't mine alone: it was shared, divvied up among the huge crowd. As we relived each decisive moment of France–Argentina, thinking of those 2 centimetres which could have changed everything, I was sometimes able to tell myself that at least I had already won a World Cup final, and that it would have been awful to have lost that one without knowing if I would have the opportunity to win one later. So I wished that all those

FINAL NIGHT

who weren't with us in rainy Moscow in 2018, showered with golden confetti, would get another chance.

I returned to London on the Tuesday morning, not knowing if I would ever play for France again. The night before, I'd confided in Franck Raviot (our goalie coach since 2010) for the first time: 'Franck, there's a good chance this final was my last match with Les Bleus.'

'This isn't the moment to be taking such hasty decisions, Hugo. Spend some time with your family, let yourself digest it all.'

Back in London with my family, I hadn't heard so much as a whisper from my club, Tottenham. Throughout the competition, I'd received regular messages from my former coaches, Mauricio Pochettino and José Mourinho, but nothing from Antonio Conte, my current manager. Not one word of encouragement, or even consolation after the final. I texted him:

'Coach, when should I return?'

'How long do you need?'

'Honestly, ten days, coach. If that's too much, we could say a few days now and a few days in January.'

'Look, we've got a Premier League match at Brentford next Monday. It would be good for the team if you turned up Sunday for training. Monday, you'll be on the bench, to ease back into it.'

EARNING MY SPURS

So turn up I did, but it was hardly 'easing back into it'. Christmas Day, a Sunday, saw me back at the ground less than a week after 36 days of intense preparation and international competition. I needed to recover from the greatest disappointment and the greatest fatigue of my career. The club gave me just four full days to do it. And I loved those four days. I managed to spend them unburdened by sadness. We ate out as a family, went for a walk in the park; my big sister Sabrina came over with my niece Paloma; it was a wonderful Christmas. I took refuge in that bubble. I set everything else aside and I refused to think about what was next. Christmas Eve was great and the kids were happy. But I headed off for training on the morning of 25 December and barely had time to drop by the house at lunchtime before returning for pre-match prep. And I remember exactly what I was thinking as I arrived at our Brentford hotel around 6 p.m., before our match the next day, where I'd be a substitute, a week after losing a World Cup final: 'What on earth am I doing here?'

II

Decision Time

The 26th of December is both Boxing Day and my birthday. I celebrated it in my tracksuit at Brentford, where we drew 2–2. From the bench, I managed to summon up a bit of interest in the match. I'd actually been quite pleased to see the guys again the previous day after such a long time. It was a happy moment, like the start of the new school year after the summer holidays. But I found players who were even more exhausted than I was. Their state affected my morale. The World Cup had worn me out and frayed my nerves, and I was counting on them to lift me up. During the half-hour video session before the match, I couldn't concentrate. My mind was simply elsewhere.

Tottenham alone wasn't responsible for my personal fog. Neither was the final, in fact. Since my return from Doha, I'd been thinking about my future with the French national team. After more than 13 years with Les Bleus, 145 caps,

DECISION TIME

four World Cups (2010, 2014, 2018, 2022) and three Euros (2012, 2016, 2021), I had to decide whether, at the age of 36, the time to turn the page had come.

Back at home, we rang in the New Year a day early, as we had so many times before. New Year's Eve saw us in pre-match prep at the Lodge – Spurs' training centre, where each player has their own room – and on 1 January I played for the first time since returning from Doha, against Aston Villa at the Tottenham Hotspur Stadium. I was still in a complete daze. I needed my teammates' energy, but they didn't have any either. At the match, I saw Emiliano Martínez, Argentina's goalie. He was a sub, having been given more days off than me, but he came and shook my hand in the tunnel before kick-off and after the final whistle too. I respect goalies, out of principle, even though I know full well that in Doha, Martínez didn't respect everyone. We even had an exchange about it in the press. In an interview with French sports daily *L'Équipe* a few days after the final, I said, 'Pratting about in goal, clearly trying to put off your opponent with behaviour that crosses a line, that's not my bag. I'm too rational, too honest to involve myself in that sort of thing.' A few weeks later he shot back in *France Football*: 'He only said that because he lost, otherwise he would have said nothing. I respect his opinion, of course. I have never insulted him. If he thinks that dancing about or gaining a bit of time constitutes a lack of respect or being dishonest, I don't share that view. Every detail counts. I give everything for my country and it won't please everyone.' I also give everything for my country. I was a little hurt by his response at first, but not that much upon reflection. Still, I have the right to think that he went too far in his behaviour against Aurélien Tchouaméni, and that his celebration with the best goalkeeper trophy was quite vulgar. That he sets out to throw off his opponent during a shootout, it's not for me to judge, but when you reach the stage where FIFA is forced to change the rules afterwards ... well, then I do judge. Walking up to Aurélien Tchouaméni, then throwing the ball away after making as if to hand it to him, yep, I judge, even though he might reply that the trick worked. Likewise, when he made a phallic gesture with the Golden Glove trophy: his celebration had a negative impact the world over, and as a de facto representative of other goalies, not to mention role model for the keepers of tomorrow, he is accountable for his actions. But he's obviously a very good goalie who made decisive saves that helped Argentina become world champions and win the Copa América.

That day, with Tottenham, the first day of 2023, I was caught off guard by a rebound and I let in a silly goal. I respected Conte's decision to select me so soon, but that

DECISION TIME

goal was tough to digest, all the same. Three days later, we won against Crystal Palace; I played well this time, but I felt like I was fighting with myself, that everything had become hard, that I had to move mountains to accomplish really simple things.

At the end of the match, I ran into Patrick Vieira, who was the Palace manager at the time. We've known each other for ages and I have a high appreciation of him. He was a world champion, too, and my first captain in the French team. We chatted about 'Les Bleus' for a few minutes, and the possibility of my retirement from international football. He was insistent: 'Continue. Above all, don't stop, if you can ...'

Before the World Cup final, I hadn't mentioned the subject of my international retirement to anyone. The idea had briefly gone through my mind during Euro 2021, following our elimination in the round of 16 against Switzerland. Like some sort of foreshadowing, we were 3–3 at full time, followed by extra time, followed by a penalty shootout which we lost (rendering my penalty save in normal time almost pointless). At 35, it was time to consider my track record. It's incredible, the energy required to play for the national team, particularly as captain. But I'd decided that I still had objectives in mind: there was the UEFA Nations League the following autumn, Lilian Thuram's record of

142 caps to beat and, of course, the World Cup in 2022. I have always used objectives to progress. In the months preceding Qatar, I was careful with my replies every time I was asked about my future, because you never know what tomorrow will bring, not to mention that I wasn't quite sure what I really wanted. As the World Cup drew closer, I stopped thinking about all this, figuring that one shouldn't announce anything before a big tournament. And since I wasn't going to announce anything, I didn't have to make a decision.

After the final, my international future became a subject of conversation for my intimate circle. I had the feeling of having reached the end of something, and the desire to leave was higher than it had ever been. I was fed up with missing those simple everyday things in my children's lives. Anna-Rose was 13 already; it all went so fast. I didn't want to be away so much, or for so long, and the reality of ageing is that recovery after a big match is tougher for me now than it used to be. Each morning it hurts as I walk downstairs to the kitchen. Every sportsperson learns to live with pain. For me, it's my lower back that tends to play up – more specifically the left-hand side these past few years – no doubt because I've been diving to the ground since I was eight. It's not so much the training itself, or the 48 hours needed to recover from a tough session, which eventually

DECISION TIME

wore me out, but successive matches, the pressure, the media focus, the essential victory – all this, every three days, as the sole horizon.

I recall training in Qatar one day, on a small pitch, when Ousmane Dembélé was on fire. He was so fast, so fluid, that he slotted two goals past me. When the session was done, I shouted, 'It's a little prick like you who'll put me out to grass!' I was laughing, but in the end he was one of the first people I told. When I finally took my decision to leave the French team, I'd already thought it through. I immediately felt freer, as if a weight had been lifted from me. I remembered how tough it was to begin with, and then: happier days. It was also the case that the national team didn't belong to me. It wasn't merely a question of age: it was time to let the next generation take their place. I didn't want to wait until I was going downhill. Having made my decision, I planned my announcement: an interview in *L'Équipe* and another on the 8 p.m. news on France's prime TV channel, TF1. But I wanted to tell the people closest to me first. Of course, I'd talked about it with my grandma, given what she means to me, as well as with my father. But it was still hard for them. It symbolized 14 years of history. As a footballer, you don't see your family as much as you'd like, and for my grandma, a France match was her opportunity to see her grandson. So whereas it was a relief for me to announce my retirement, all they had left was nostalgia, a little sadness that it was over, and the certainty that never again would we experience something as wonderful together as our trip to Doha, which they still talk about. My father agreed with my decision, but that doesn't mean it was easy for him.

I told Franck Raviot, the long-time goalie coach of the French national team and a man I trusted: I knew he would keep it to himself. And, of course, I told our manager, Didier Deschamps. I texted him my New Year's greetings, adding: 'If we could have a word when you've got a moment . . .' He rang me straight away. I couldn't get the words out at first. 'Go on, Hugo,' he said, 'just say what's on your mind, and then we'll see . . .' I told him, very quickly: 'Coach, I've made my decision. It won't be easy to make the announcement, but I prefer to tell you immediately, and no one will make me change my mind. I'm quitting the squad . . .' He advised me not to make an impulse decision, to wait a bit, maybe, but I explained that I'd given my all and that I didn't think I had much left in the tank. Two days later, when it was announced that his contract had been extended, I texted him: 'Congratulations, coach. I'm happy for you and all the staff. You deserve it.' He replied that they would all miss me. I told him I would miss them all too.

I got in touch with the goalies who really matter to

DECISION TIME

me: Fabien Barthez, who I'm close to and who's always supported me, as well as Joël Bats, who was my coach at Lyon – and much more besides – for four years. I told them I was thinking things over and that I wanted to know what they thought about it. Fab told me how the end had come for him, following the 2006 World Cup, as well as the time a while before when he nearly quit. As for Joël: 'You'll see,' he said. 'At first, when France were winning without me, I told myself I could still have been there. And when things went badly, I told myself that I did well to retire.' He was right. This was a fundamental question: do you still have the energy to overcome those difficult periods that teams go through? Because when you've carried the weight of expectation for so long, when you've taken blow after blow, when you've not just been the goalkeeper but captain too, there comes a time, despite the joy, the pride and the victories, when you can no longer hack it. And this time, I was done.

I made sure that Antonio Conte was informed. And I also called the Spurs chairman, Daniel Levy.

On Monday 9 January I had lunch at the offices of *L'Équipe* in the Paris suburb of Boulogne-Billancourt. The journalists from the football section who'd followed me all those years were there. And it was me who brought the champagne, of course. I'd have loved to have made my announcement at a press conference after a France match, then buy all the journalists a drink. I'd not been their best customer the day before a match – I was much chattier the day after. And they weren't always kind to me – something I'd never asked of them; they have their own role to play, after all. But journalists and players experience a sort of apprenticeship over the long haul: we travel the world together, with us at the heart of the action and them right alongside, so having a drink together seemed appropriate.

Late on that Monday afternoon, an hour before it became official, I started telling my best friends. And I let the other players know, the veterans: Antoine Griezmann, Olivier Giroud, Raphaël Varane, as well as Kylian Mbappé. It was also my way of telling them, 'Right, guys, it's up to you now.' I didn't know yet that Raphaël was quitting too. I called Kylian because I'd sensed during the World Cup that he was starting to have some clout in the dressing room, and that he was going to take over the leadership.

That Monday in Paris, I messaged Mauricio Pochettino, my longest-serving manager at Tottenham, who's part of my football family: 'How you doing, gaffer? I'm in your city. Sorry, I mean Toni Jiménez's city [a private joke: Toni's his goalie coach and loves Paris]. I wanted to let you know before it becomes official that I'm going to announce my international retirement.' I've kept his reply:

DECISION TIME

'Thanks, Hugo. I really appreciate you letting me know. I hoped to see you in the national team for ever, but I understand your decision. Family time is important. I'm proud of you, of everything you achieved with the squad. The main thing is that you're happy.'

I *had* been happy in the French team, for a long time. And I was happy to be settling things properly during those January days. The qualifying stage for Euro 2024 would start in March, so it was important for there to be no doubt hanging over my future. My sponsors and the manager needed certainty. I owed them that out of respect. There had been no passing of the baton when I joined the French team. So I wanted to ensure a handover, that there would be a legacy, that the conditions would be right for everything to continue as before. That's why I was able to leave in peace. I knew that Mike Maignan, a top-notch goalie, was waiting in the wings, that he'd be there for several years and would accomplish great things. I'd arrived in autumn 2008, an unsettled period when everyone was out for himself, though it wasn't yet a scorched-earth thing – the debacle would come a year and a half later in South Africa. It took me a long while to feel that I'd joined a true team: mates with a joint ambition.

I quit after a World Cup that would have been brilliant, but for that one regret that won't leave me, that defeat in the final after the penalty shootout. Often I tell myself that I should have stopped one, and then I realize that I should have stopped three. But I know it's not that simple either, and that if I'd stopped one at the right moment, maybe things would have been different. You never know.

It was an emotional thing to announce that I was leaving the French team. I was relieved to have made the decision, and bowled over by the reactions, be they from fans or other players. I received dozens and dozens of messages, even from certain players I didn't expect, and journalists too. Shooting an interview for TF1 in London, during which I watched clips of people's reactions and their homages, it all came back to me and I couldn't help but shed a tear. It was like a living obituary, emotionally overpowering and intense.

And so it was over. Maybe my biggest fault is having rarely appreciated things at the time, of always focusing too quickly on the future. That's a trait I get from my grandmother, who constantly looks ahead and never talks about the past. I've always looked ahead, but then one fine day, it's over. That's also just the way of competitive sport. But once I'd quit, I began appreciating better, and more fully, all of the joy and pride of those years with Les Bleus. What regrets could I have?

I had been six when I started playing for a club, the Cedac

DECISION TIME

de Cimiez, in my childhood neighbourhood in northern Nice. Training was every Wednesday and it was my grandpa who took me. He would pick me up after school on a Tuesday evening and I slept at his and my grandma's. The next morning, before my training session, we went to their bridge club at La Colle-sur-Loup west of Nice, where I carried on with my homework. Eventually I'd get changed. When I stood in front of them in my kit, my grandpa would proudly announce to his bridge buddies: 'I present the future goalkeeper of the French team.' I was eight.

III

The Void

Caps: 145; captaincies: 121; World Cup finals: two – I always knew I was privileged. The French national team has been the common thread throughout my career, even at the very start. I was an international for just over 14 years, from 8 November 2008 to 18 December 2022, and when I decided it was over, I faced a void. I expected a few tough weeks: Les Bleus symbolized so much for me that all of my torments and injuries were concentrated in the two or three months following the seven major tournaments that I played with France. Yet, in spite of all that, I would never have imagined what was now going to happen. I had even dared to think that focusing on my club game would help me perform well.

The truth is that nothing or no one helped me at this time – hardly anyone at any rate. That's how it works in football: the manager thinks that what little energy you have left will be enough to help the team. But the Premier League is relentless. The play is fast, and it's a constant battle. On 23 January 2023 at Fulham, where we won 0–1, I played a solid match, even though I still had trouble focusing during the warm-up. Craven Cottage is a lovely little stadium with a soul, and the supporters are so close they seem to envelop you; perfect for getting my competition head back on. As I was crossing the pitch at the end of the match, Cristian Stellini, Antonio Conte's assistant, called out: 'Hey, Hugo, go check with the manager, but I told him that I'd give you a five- or six-day break.' I could have done with them sooner, but the subsequent few days in Nice did me a power of good.

I felt great when I came back for the Manchester City game (1–0) at home on 5 February, probably my last really good match for Tottenham. Right at the end, I stopped a Rodri header with a flying save to my left and felt something give when my right knee hit the Spanish international. I'd been telling myself that I was back, that I'd got the machine fired up again, that the Champions League was on the horizon – the round of 16 match against AC Milan was a week later – and that I was handling myself pretty well, all things considered. But after this clearance, I realized that my stability was seriously affected. The exterior ligament of my right knee – on my supporting leg – had gone. I would be out for six to eight weeks, and so began the troubled twilight of my London years. From the World Cup final on 18 December 2022 to my departure from Tottenham on 30 December 2023, I played only ten matches with Spurs, the last ten of my 447 appearances for the club since 2012. A lifetime.

Like all injured players, I stepped away from the team to recover, returning in the spring full of beans and eager to get stuck in. But when I came back, Antonio Conte had been sacked and the atmosphere was abysmal. The whole team was listless. If a collective is strong, you can underperform and no one will notice. At Tottenham, everything was visible. I started to visualize the end of a phase of my life, and my objective became to finish the season, to dedicate myself to my club and to think of a place where I could enjoy myself again. I'd always thought that with six weeks' holiday in summer and taking it easy during the international breaks, I could extend my career pretty easily. But after my knee there came another injury, a tendon that went as I cleared the ball during the first half of a nightmarish Spurs game at Newcastle in April, which we lost 6–1. It was my last match with the club.

Once I'd reached the age of 30, major competitions always had an effect on my athletic and mental health, and I wasn't alone in being deeply affected, both physically and emotionally, by this World Cup right in the middle of the season.

THE VOID

Some players were ghosts of themselves in the second part of the season, while others were injured, as I was.

My lassitude never really tipped into depression. There was massive burnout, sure, after such intense and sometimes contradictory emotions, but no unjustified sadness. It was simply that nothing was light or fluid any more. Even in the past, when I'd had three weeks to recover from a World Cup or a Euros, I would injure myself out of fatigue or because I threw myself back into it too hard and too fast – the job and my managers having demanded it. Being on the bench for a Premier League fixture a week after the World Cup final was absurd. As was the scheduling of league fixtures just a week before the World Cup began.

I'd left the French team in January 2023; by May I'd started wondering about quitting Tottenham too. I was only thinking about it, though, not expecting that Spurs would make a move so quickly. But in preparation for what they clearly saw as my impending departure, the club hired another goalkeeper, the Italian Guglielmo Vicario. The message to me was all too clear: having been captain of the team for ten years, I was no longer a part of their plans. Before the summer tour of the US, I asked the chairman, Daniel Levy, if I really had to join everyone on this tour to promote a club which didn't want me any more. His answer was that I could stay behind in London.

I always knew, of course, that such a moment would come. What I didn't appreciate, though, was them letting me know at the end of the season, when it was already very late to sort myself out in what was quite a closed goalie market. But there was more to it than my simply wanting to go. Following a recurring rumour in late May that I was off to Saudi Arabia (I had only been contacted by some agents), Daniel Levy summoned me. As we talked, I quickly realized that my supposed departure would suit him. We went over the season together. I told him what I thought of the situation at the club, and he ended up telling me of the club's wish to buy a much younger first-team keeper. He even suggested I make my farewells at Spurs' last home match. To which I replied:

'But I've got a year's contract left, Daniel, who knows what might happen?'

'I wouldn't like you to leave like that, Hugo, after all these seasons with us, everything you've done for the club. I'd like to pay you a homage.'

'We're not going to do a homage at a last match, at the end of our worst season, when we might not even qualify for the European Cup ...'

In mentioning the recruitment of a younger keeper, Daniel was letting me understand that the club would not ask to be compensated for the final year of my contract.

THE VOID

But I had a salary which few clubs could meet, and which Tottenham would have liked to reduce, and, at 36, after a second half of the season with two injuries and a certain irregularity in appearances and results, I felt that the club wished to turn the page. In the end, I saw this situation as an opening, a way out. I just would have liked, yet again, to have known earlier: they'd already chosen the new keeper weeks before, but had decided not to tell me.

I saw Daniel Levy again in August, when he tried to convince me to go to Lazio. But although I was touched by the approach from Lazio's chairman, Claudio Lotito, whom I'd met in the past, I didn't really see the point in leaving for a club which already had a first-team keeper, Ivan Provedel, and risk holding back a goalie who was progressing really well and had had an excellent season. I didn't need that. We're more than just assets: we're men, with families, children. Were I younger, I might have gone. But not now.

I stayed at Tottenham because, just a few hours from the end of the transfer window, I didn't want to be rushed into making a decision without having time to think it over. Whenever I move anywhere, four others move with me. So while rumours were rife of my imminent transfer to Newcastle as number 2 goalie – or of my return to Nice – I enjoyed a peaceful family dinner at an Argentinian restaurant in Hampstead.

EARNING MY SPURS

Once the transfer window had closed, I very quickly realized that I would pay a price for this attitude, as I became a Tottenham player who didn't play any more, who didn't exist in his own club. I never said anything, no one ever heard me complain, but all too often I found that I simply couldn't stand the situation any longer. At times I was really close to throwing in the towel and ripping up the contract which tied me to the club until June 2024. And this was a club, after all, where I had spent 12 seasons – nine of which as captain – a total of 447 matches in the Spurs strip.

On my better days I put myself in the shoes of Ange Postecoglou, the new manager, who'd arrived at a club that had hired a young goalie and was commencing a new phase. It was logical that he follow this new direction. All of the outfield players who were in the same situation as me, who the club wanted to get rid of, reintegrated into the team and had to compete with each other as usual. But it's not the same for keepers. Even if I'd done what was required in training to perform properly, I wouldn't have played again because it's a position which requires stability and conviction. If there is any competitiveness at all, then it is over the very long term, from one season to the next, sometimes from one contract to the next, but never from match to match. A goalkeeper who has one bad game is replaced only on the rarest occasions, if ever.

THE VOID

The break did me good at first, as if time was paused. I was training with a team I was no longer a part of, and would never be again, whatever happened. I joined in the training sessions requiring four goalies, but the opposed practice sessions which required only two keepers were not for me. I had never been in such a situation and I could never have imagined it. I'm not cut out for that sort of thing.

When the guys needed a keeper to blast away at, I was that man, just like when I was 18, because I missed playing and jumped at any opportunity to get my hands on the ball. But I yearned for all the other stuff, particularly matches, even practice sessions, on a big pitch with space. This period confirmed something I've long believed: that there are practice goalies, good 'shot-stoppers', but a real goalie is one who knows how to read the game well and handle the whole pitch, his penalty area and his defence. Working the goalline is just one aspect of the role, and I was no longer a complete keeper if that was all I did during close-play sessions and isolated exercises.

It was a terrible autumn and it ate away at me. I observed, sometimes amused, often saddened, the social consequences in the dressing room of my demotion from captain to invisible player. A few people followed the logic of the firm: since the club had decided to sideline me (even if it was more complicated than that), they sidelined me too.

Relations shouldn't change for such a reason. I was disappointed that some players avoided me like the plague. I was no longer a part of the team; the manager never spoke to me and there was no way I was going to be interested in his presentations on matches that I wouldn't be playing in. As long as I stay in football, I will always try to remember to maintain a connection with everyone. This simply was not the case during my last six months at Spurs.

I didn't want to be stuck there in the middle any more. I wanted to extricate myself. This is precisely what I said to my family when I got home following the debrief of our 2–1 defeat by West Ham in early December 2023: 'I've got to get out of here, I can't take it any longer. When everything's going well for the team, I'm not happy because I'm excluded from it; and when everything's going badly for them, I'm not happy either because it's my club and I'm attached to it.' I hated that feeling of being caught between two equally uncomfortable stools, one in the stands, the other mounted on an ejector seat.

But throughout this whole period I never had a single negative thought for Guglielmo Vicario, the goalie playing in my stead. Guglielmo is a serious, respectful, hardworking guy who had absolutely nothing to do with the situation I was put in. It would have been tough for me to take otherwise. He came to this level of play somewhat late, at the age of 27, after only two seasons in Serie A, but he knows what he wants, and he's a grafter – he even goes to the ground on his days off to do his stretching exercises. I think he'll go far. He deserves to.

Although I kept up a social life with my former teammates, I avoided the team meals because I was the former captain and I needed to let the group gel without me.

I made good use of the time, though, spending it with my children or managing other areas of my life, such as my financial assets. Approaching the end of my football career, I naturally sought to plan for the next stage of my life.

It wasn't until winter 2023, when I took the decision to become a proper player again (but elsewhere), that I started to miss the adrenaline rush. I watched matches often, but there wasn't a single one where I said to myself that I would have liked to be there. I didn't identify with anything: the French national team was the past, and Tottenham was my team no longer. For the first time, I was faced with the reality that there was more to life than football. I have never been scared of stopping completely, and it's possible that if the World Cup had taken place in June 2022, rather than in December, I would have hung up my gloves then.

That autumn, when I felt invisible and useless, I detached myself from the team because it was the best way to protect myself. That's why I didn't visit the stadium from June to

September. I was no longer a player, really, but not yet a spectator either. I always knew that I would become an unconditional Tottenham fan again the very day I left, but I had to find the proper distance during that autumn, like a separated couple who still live in the same house.

For several months I was convinced that my bosses were going to mess up my exit. I thought, and still do, that if they wanted to be rid of me in summer 2023, they should have sat me down and come to an amicable arrangement regarding my departure. We never entered into the slightest negotiation; they just wanted me out. In summer 2021, when the Italian Fabio Paratici took over as director of football, I had had an inkling that something was afoot. I was one year out from the end of my contract, and not only had they still not made me an offer (which set the rumour mill whirring all summer), but they'd brought in an Italian goalkeeper, Pierluigi Gollini. But with my sights set on the World Cup a year later, I continued to perform at a high level; so after Antonio Conte took over the team in November, he had my contract extended within a couple of months. The tables had turned and now I had the upper hand: the club had been forced to show me some respect, as we say in footie now when a club accepts a player's conditions without negotiating. So, yes, I disliked those long eight months at Tottenham without playing. I disliked

THE VOID

that novel feeling of being invisible in a club which meant so much to me. And I disliked being useless and feeling surplus to requirements. Over the course of those months, which seemed like years, I often thought that my Spurs story deserved a different ending, a beautiful one. But I was wrong to doubt. I now know that the end was indeed beautiful. That's a story for another time, though.

IV

'I Think I Want to Quit, Dad'

I'm a child of the Mediterranean. My roots extend across its rim on each side. I was born and grew up in Nice, which will always be *my* town. My paternal grandparents came from Algeria and Morocco and I was lucky to have them for so many years. Out of us three children (my older sister Sabrina and younger brother Gautier), I was the one who got to spend the most time with them. My grandfather took me everywhere: to football matches and practice sessions, and in the summer holidays they took me on the road in their camper van. We always started by spending two or three weeks at Cap d'Agde because my grandfather worked for the state electric company which had a number of holiday apartments in the resort for employees' use. Next, we'd roam across the bottom

'I THINK I WANT TO QUIT, DAD'

half of France, although we did once drive as far as the Pointe du Raz at the tip of Brittany. The whole trip could last five weeks. My brother came along once, to Sète, but the camper van had gone by then.

My paternal grandpa was born in Lille, but grew up in Algeria, in Mers el-Kébir, where my father was born. My grandpa's sister lived in Meknes, in Morocco, which is where my grandpa met my grandma, who had grown up there. They lived together in Meknes, before moving to France when my father was 20. I thought about these roots, of course, when we beat Morocco in the semi-finals of the 2022 World Cup, but I was already aware of this history and these origins as a child. At school or footie, when guys from the other side of the Med learned about my roots, they saw me almost as a member of their family.

Lloris is a Catalan name, but you have to go a long way back in my family tree to find a Catalan ancestor. My grandma's maiden name was Crespo – this is why I always liked Hernán Crespo, the former Parma and Argentina centre-forward. In fact, I've always loved Argentinian players, although their nationality was almost coincidental: if I was a fan of Crespo, Gabriel Batistuta and Claudio López, it wasn't because they were Argentinian, but because I loved the Valencia team of the late 1990s, and its goalie, Santiago Cañizares – and, in the case of Batistuta, Fiorentina, with its beautiful purple strip and, of course, its keeper, Francesco Toldo.

As close as I was to my paternal grandparents growing up, I never knew my maternal ones, who died before I was born. However, I did know my maternal great-grandparents, César and Marthe, who lived in Aix-en-Provence. We would go to visit them once a month.

My mum, Christine Demanget, met my dad, Luc Lloris, in Aix-en-Provence when they were students – my mum had to break off her degree when she was expecting my sister, Sabrina, who was two or three when my father finished his politics studies. They left Aix to go and live with my father's parents in Beausoleil, next to Monaco, for a year, before finally having enough cash to get their own apartment on Avenue Henry Dunant in the northern part of Nice. That's where I got to know the family of my friend Cédric Messina (the founder of the MyCoach personal fitness app) who lived 200 metres from us. I spent a lot of time at Marcel and Danielle's with their three kids, Warren (who's two years older than me), David and Cédric. Danielle, or 'Dada', was our nanny: first my sister's, then mine and finally my brother's. I performed my first real dives in the corridors of their apartment. Warren and I played in the corridor every night in our socks, using a foam ball, slipping and sliding, bashing into the walls, and

'I THINK I WANT TO QUIT, DAD'

breaking stuff on occasion. I always escaped unscathed, but one day, years later, I had to go with my dad to collect my little brother who was bleeding from his head, and take him to the Lenval children's hospital. He still has the scar behind his ear. We also played at home, of course, and our relentless matches ended up smashing both a collector's mug belonging to my great-grandma and a windowpane. And with me being the eldest of us two boys, I was the one who copped it. We were obliged to keep a low profile for a few days, so we headed downstairs to the lawn outside the building to play, the yells of 'Keep off the grass!' from the old folks ringing in our ears. If we'd listened to them all, we'd never have played anywhere.

As little kids in Nice we spent every weekend at the Tennis Club des Combes. I was wielding a racket and a yellow ball from as soon as I could walk. Even then, I dived after every shot when we played on the grass next to the courts. It was a lively place, with a soul. Most of the people came for the day, like we did: my dad played with his mates in the morning, with my mother in the afternoon, and in between we had lunch in the club restaurant, which was run by a couple, France and Henri. It was thanks to Henri, who was a friend of Régis Bruneton – a midfielder for Marseille and Toulouse in the 1950s and 1960s, and my first coach – that I signed for Cedac de Cimiez in 1993, at the tender age of six. I recall my first visit there vividly. Decked out in my beautiful yellow strip, gloves and everything, I went to introduce myself to Régis Bruneton: 'Hi, Régis, my name is Hugo. Henri said to come. I'm a goalkeeper.'

I know what's been said about me, but claiming that I come from a wealthy background does not reflect the reality. My parents moved up in the world, it's true, but through hard work. They did loads of odd jobs. My mum, who was born in Bordeaux but grew up in Fontainebleau, just outside Paris, was a very bright pupil who passed her *baccalauréat* early, aged 16; but she also worked in a patisserie, then at a law firm: initially as receptionist, then as project manager, before gaining her qualifications to become a legal advisor. She also taught management and English. My father, who was a maths and economics teacher, and who also worked in the management office of the Le Méridien hotel on the Promenade des Anglais, started out on the bottom rung in a bank, the CMB Monaco, before rising up the ranks to become an executive and working in three different banks. My parents worked so much that my sister left home at 15, spending the week in a boarding school outside Paris, and staying with my uncle Dominique at weekends. I remember our childhood with her thanks to photos, mainly. I was four or five years old when she left, and I inherited her room in our small apartment. I recall

'I THINK I WANT TO QUIT, DAD'

her leaving then coming back sometimes, without really understanding what was going on, but I was happy when she spent a few days in Nice with us. Sabrina lived in Paris for a long time, where she gave birth to Emilio, my nephew, before moving to Bourges, where my niece Paloma was born, then to Toulouse and finally 80 kilometres east to Castres. Emilio is 24 now and totally rugby mad. The absence I felt at my sister's sudden departure was somewhat compensated by the presence of my grandparents, who had left Beausoleil for the western Nice neighbourhood of La Madeleine, before settling a little further west on the main road (the RN 202) that runs along the left bank of the River Var. That's where I always remember them being. Their apartment became my bolthole after football practice. Later on, Gautier even lived with my grandma for a year in order to be closer to the training centre and avoid all that travel back and forth.

My childhood was not that of a banker's son, as people have described it since, although my parents did manage to change their lives and increase their income over the years, after many sacrifices. It took them nearly two decades to move out of our neighbourhood in northern Nice and buy an apartment in Fabron, closer to the sea. I was 11 when we moved, in the middle of the school year. My parents worked hard for us, and during the winter holidays my mum would book us a week's skiing in Tignes, Val-d'Isère or La Plagne. In summer, it might be a week at Club Med in Chamonix. She loved going away with us so much that it would become an issue later, when I started going on pre-season training camps with my club. My first one was over near Manosque, in Provence, when I was 15. Up until then, I'd been able to say that I wasn't available for regular training and could therefore go on holiday with my family for a week. My coaches at Nice, Gérard Buscher and Alain Wathelet, were understanding for as long as they could be, but there came a point when it clearly wasn't working any more. The first time I had to miss the family holiday, it was my dad who spoke to my mum about it – I would have found it too hard to negotiate myself. Their discussion was a tense one, but I get it now: this marked the end of childhood in their eyes, and football, which was of little interest to my mum, was taking her son away from her at *the* moment in the year she looked forward to most. The following winter, we had to renegotiate all over again. The truth was that my mum didn't like the negative environment around football, all the pressure from parents, fans and coaches. With hindsight, I understand more what she felt, as well as her fears: I've felt ill at ease myself, those few times I've been to watch Gautier train, picking up on the concerns and tensions of the parents from their body language and how they talk. This wasn't my mother's idea of sport. Deep down it bothered her that I was playing footie, but when I turned professional, I knew that she followed my career closely and was proud of me.

Watching matches at home required some guile on occasion. Having only the one telly, on Champions League nights we had to wait until my mother had gone to sleep to watch the second half. Weekends were different: I didn't watch the games on TV because I was playing most of the time. The Champions League was my thing, and whenever that coincided with me spending the evening at my grandparents, after school or training, I would watch the first half with my grandpa before rushing home where, if I'd done my homework and my mum was ready for bed, I had a chance of seeing the second.

I was a good student most of the time, except for a term at the Collège Raoul Dufy (in a western neighbourhood of Nice) when I was 11 and still living in the north of Nice. It was the one disastrous period in all my school years. As a little kid, I loved going to Rosalinde Rancher primary school, where my big sister had gone, and Gautier too for a while. When I was ten I was lucky to have a wonderful teacher, Monsieur Joly, who was strict yet fun, with huge glasses, and who knew how to get kids to join in. Each playtime, he'd hand out ping-pong paddles and we'd play with him, or else he'd give us a foam football and we'd organize a tournament. I also had a penchant for rummaging through my father's pockets for a ten-franc coin to buy Panini stickers, Pogs or marbles. I didn't buy many CDs, and books were something I only got into when I was older. I realize now that what I'm going through with my kids is what my parents went through with me. Sometimes, when I see them in front of a screen, I'll say, 'Enough with screens, pick up a book!' I know I didn't always listen to my parents, but Marine and I are pretty firm on limiting screen-time.

Looking back, I don't really know why I chose football. It wasn't a family affair, at least not until my grandpa got involved. My father played tennis. He was ranked highly, played team competitions on weekends, and I loved watching him on the court. I turned towards football of my own volition, although my grandma tells me that I used to kick a ball about on their balcony and that I yelled if no one passed it to me. And it turns out that my grandpa had a thing for goalies. He would tell me about Georges Carnus, the former keeper of AS Saint-Étienne, Olympique de Marseille and the French national team, who had me do some individual training one day (when I was playing in the Ligue Méditerranée) with Bruno Bini, who was in charge

'I THINK I WANT TO QUIT, DAD'

of selection and a future coach of the French national women's team.

Sport took up my entire childhood. It was a hobby I was passionate about, but never did I imagine a future as a professional. I just wanted to play, that's all. At Cimiez the pitch was so short that I tried to score from goalkicks and clearances, and succeeded a handful of times; and if I got too bored, or if we were behind, I'd play in the outfield – Régis Bruneton, the coach, was OK with this because I was fast and had a good left foot.

But my grandpa had ambitions for me, there's no doubt. One summer, when we were still living in the north of Nice and no one was even talking about moving to the western part of town yet, I was at his place when he read an advert in the regional newspaper *Nice-Matin* for a scouting session at Olympique Gymnaste Club de Nice, commonly known as OGC Nice. I was nine. He didn't even mention it to my parents, just signed me up, and because it was the holidays, I had nothing better to do. There were six of us goalies and the programme included a session with Dominique Baratelli, a former keeper of Nice, Paris Saint-Germain (PSG) and the French national team, who had played in the 1978 and 1982 World Cups. At the end of the day-long session, he announced: 'The young'un's got potential.' The Nice coaches wanted me to sign for the coming season right off the bat, but it was impossible, I lived too far away. So I stayed at Cimiez. But the following summer, my grandpa took me to the same scouting session again, but as an outfield player this time, having played as a striker at Cimiez all season, in the first year of juniors. But although I was often the best scorer in tournaments, and had great pace, my future as a centre-forward came to an abrupt end when Dominique Baratelli recognized me from the previous year and shouted, 'No, no! Put the gloves back on, you!'

This time, we said yes to OGC Nice. It was the second year of juniors: five training sessions a week and a match on weekends. I would soon forsake tennis, having delivered several fine performances in team competitions and holiday tournaments against adults. I believe I even played a couple of finals, but didn't win.

The truth is that I wasn't too happy during my first seasons at Nice. I was only ten, but already we were being put upon to win because we were OGC Nice - so much for the pleasure of playing. I'd come from a neighbourhood club where I'd been enjoying myself, and suddenly this was serious business. The first difficulties came the next year. Having started in the second team with the under-13s, I wasn't playing much and injured myself. I just wasn't physically conditioned yet. Stepping up from the small pitch to the big pitch, I found I couldn't take a proper goalkick

'I THINK I WANT TO QUIT, DAD'

because I couldn't even get the ball to the centre-line. I tore an adductor muscle on a kick and couldn't play for two months. When I returned, another kid was in goal. They clearly didn't believe in me and I wanted to jack it all in. I have never forgotten the conversation I had with my dad in the car. I was 12 and it was a difficult time because we'd moved the previous year, I'd received a warning about my work from school, and my grandpa was putting a huge amount of pressure on me. 'I think I want to quit, Papa,' I said to my dad. I lacked the vocabulary to explain what I was feeling, but what it boiled down to was that I wasn't fulfilled. I'd come from little old Cedac de Cimiez, where football was a game, and I didn't like the atmosphere at OGC Nice where even the coaches were under pressure. I wasn't ready for that. My father listened to me, then simply said, 'Finish the season, and then you'll see.' I hadn't yet completely given up on tennis. I was unsure what I wanted, but this conversation suddenly lifted a weight off me: I no longer felt constrained, since he was leaving it up to me to choose, when the time was right. I actually had a very strong end to the season, and it all took off from there. What's more, the coach of the second team, Pascal Herbette, was being moved up to the first team the following season. He'd trusted me, and I smashed it, picking up selections for the Ligue Méditerranée and then in turn the national under-15s and under-17s, playing with guys who were two years older than me. It just goes to show the benefits of not keeping things to yourself, of saying what's on your mind sometimes, even with few words. Nothing has ever been easy in my development, but in sport at the highest level the only way to get there and to stay there is to fight for it every step of the way.

The pressure from my grandpa remained considerable. He was an emotional chap and his temperament would get the better of him. When I played a good match, he would talk to me about it for hours, proud as could be. But when I played a bad match, he would react negatively. I was enveloped in my grandparents' love, but sometimes found it suffocating, particularly Grandpa's. From my very first year in juniors, Grandma would cut out and keep everything, even just the team-results listing in *Nice-Matin*, while Grandpa came to all the OGC Nice training sessions at the pitch adjoining the Stade du Ray, where he would comment on everything. Whenever I made a save, even an easy one, he would shout, 'Great save, well done!' But if I let a ball go, I would get a resounding, 'Don't let the ball go!' Grandpa would continue his critiques in the car afterwards, picking apart my errors in as much length as he extolled my feats. The drive home took ages sometimes. I never made him so proud as during one particularly insane Monaco–Nice

'I THINK I WANT TO QUIT, DAD'

under-15s match, which we drew 0–0: he talked to me about it for weeks. His reproaches were as intense as his pride. I hold very tender memories of it all now, but as a teenager it was also something I tried to escape from.

As I grew older, and progressed in my abilities, I never wondered if I was good at football or better than the rest. I tried only to live up to my grandpa's expectations. Even recognition by others didn't satisfy me. And when I started playing for regional teams, that wasn't enough for me either. The real tipping point would come the day I started training with the pros. Up until then, footie was just my very serious pastime and source of enjoyment, for I was equally devoted to my schoolwork. And if I didn't have much free time between academic swotting and football practice, well, that's just the way I evolved. Deep down, my goalkeeper's temperament was already in place. I was conscientious and disciplined, but couldn't keep still either. I remember climbing up onto the roof of the tennis clubhouse one day to retrieve a ball (five metres off the ground) and falling through the skylight into the storeroom belonging to Patrice (who ran the club shop), and landing on my feet like a cat – or nearly: I cut open my head and elbow and still have the scars. The main thing I recall from that incident is my father buying me a huge chocolate *macaron* on the way back from hospital as a reward for being so intrepid, after he'd been scared stiff that I'd really hurt myself.

I worked hard at school and I worked hard at football. In my second year at Nice, in the under-13s, I started taking proper goalkicks. For ages, Grandpa had been yelling at me from his usual spot behind me because I hadn't managed to do it. We played on packed-sand or artificial pitches, and it was hard to get my foot under the ball, but I practised and practised, and eventually was able to reach the centre-line. Tall and skinny, with my pudding basin haircut, Baratelli said that I looked like a Russian keeper.

For a long time I didn't have a dedicated goalie coach, but I've never forgotten Didier Veschi – an amazing instructor for anyone learning the role – who would sometimes end the sessions with a rugby ball to make us work on our reflexes after it bounced, or with aerial balls which he'd send soaring. As basic as that might seem today, it was all new to us then. He taught us to dive, then get up again. Didier had been an amateur goalie and he used to say that a really good keeper shouldn't need to dive. I've always remembered that. There was Abdallah Bah, too – a keeper with Nice B who even had a loan spell with Leyton Orient – whom I adored; he coached the under-17s. Training with him was a delight.

I was first capped for the under-18s French team when

'I THINK I WANT TO QUIT, DAD'

I was still at high school, where I followed the usual curriculum. My teammates attended either a regional training centre or else the prestigious national one at Clairefontaine. They included Yohan Cabaye, Younès Kaboul, Yoann Gourcuff, Didier Digard and Abou Diaby, one of the strongest players I've ever encountered, but whose career was plagued by injuries, sadly. In 2003 I played and won my first international match in Germany (0–1), before my final school exams. In a TV report many years later, my maths teacher at the time confessed that up until my absence for that selection he had no idea that I was a footballer, and neither did the other teachers.

I wanted to take the economics stream at high school, as my father had done, but he advised me to take the science one instead, saying that it would give me more choice career-wise. Professional footballer was clearly not a family ambition. But I loved high school. I had an amazing set of classmates in my final two years, and it was my best time as regards juggling schoolwork and football. I had two mates in particular: Stéphane, who remains a close friend; and Jean-Marc, whom I don't see so often but who I would hang out with all the time back then. I had no issue keeping up with my studies, but the closer it got to final exams, the more I had to make strategic choices. I had an overloaded schedule, with a mainstream school timetable and no special arrangements, but I loved that it was a mad dash to fit it all in: training, lessons, family, friends. That period helped me to channel my energy, and even though to this day I still have the need to keep busy, I'm rather more serene. I was pretty decent at maths, no issues at all, and science likewise. But as the final exams approached, my father didn't want to leave anything to chance and paid for extra maths tuition on Saturday mornings, from ten till 12, since that was the only time in the week I wasn't doing anything. It was a small class, I quite liked it, and, what's more, if the weekend match was on Sunday, I could grab some lunch in town and go and see a film. If I was playing that afternoon, then my dad would pick me up and we'd rush to the match. Always against the clock.

At high school, I kept the same friends from middle school: Rok, Anthony, Stéphane. And they're still here, they keep me rooted. I've got loads of mates inside and outside football, good friends too, but those relationships can never be the same. The start of the story cannot be erased. A little while ago, after a day out on the water, I ran into John, a guy who was in high school with me. He works in finance now, and we'd not seen each other for 20 years, but it was as if we'd said goodbye the previous day – we talked about the same things, in the same way. High school is also where I met Marine.

V

'Go For it, it's All Yours!'

I passed my exams in June 2004, having led a double life: revising while playing the semi-finals and final of the under-18s French championship. School was barely over when the former Monaco and Nice midfielder Roger Ricort – who would become the OGC Nice director of sport – told me that training with the B team would pick up again in mid-July. 'No,' I shot back, 'I want to join the pros.' And so it was agreed with the chairman, Maurice Cohen. I got what I wanted, but now there were four goalies in the pros – Damien Grégorini, Bruno Valencony, Hilaire Muñoz and me – and even though I did some long individual practice sessions with Enrico Pionetti, the first-team goalkeeping coach, I didn't take part in many of the pre-season sessions. In September I decided to stop training with them in

'GO FOR IT, IT'S ALL YOURS!'

order to play with the B team again. It was a tricky move because, as the number 3 goalie of the pros, returning to play with the B team in order to get back into the swing of things meant relegation to the under-18s, and this held me back just when I'd decided to devote myself entirely to football for the first time. Having recently finished school, my life was now somewhat lacking. Fortunately everything changed in January, and quickly: Hilaire Muñoz had left on loan and Bruno Valencony got injured at the end of a practice session the day before a French Cup match, resulting in me being picked to line up with the pros and having to join them for pre-match prep. I dashed home to pack my stuff while the pros drove to Carros (a few kilometres north of Nice) for the prep. I'd just turned 18 and didn't have my driving licence yet, so it was my grandma who drove me to the hotel, where I was surprised not to find anyone. It turned out that the meeting point was at a restaurant a little way away. When I showed up, the whole team clapped me – the usual welcome reserved for latecomers. Some debut.

January 2005 also marked the first time I took my place on a bench in Ligue 1, against Lille and my mate Yohan Cabaye. It was a first glimpse and a good introduction to senior football, enabling me to see up close how things were done in a professional dressing room before a match, and how fast the play was. I took it all in, discovering the match-day rituals. To my young eyes, everything seemed to take an inordinately long time. Later, I would come to appreciate how the gentle pace of things before and after a match helped you recuperate.

In April, as we teetered on the brink of relegation, I became the number 2 keeper and was picked as a sub against PSG at Parc des Princes – a result of Bruno Valencony's injury. We lost that match, and four days later Gernot Rohr was replaced as manager by Gérard Buscher, my former coach in the juniors. The club was saved with two days to go by a decisive goal against Ajaccio from the striker Kamel Larbi. With Buscher, who'd confirmed my number 2 place, we took eight points out of 12 to avoid the drop.

That summer I made the acquaintance of David Ginola. Late in the season, Olivier Echouafni, a stalwart of the team, asked me to take part in a beach soccer tournament in Sainte-Maxime, just across the gulf from Saint-Tropez. David was the organizer and there were some really good players present, such as Jimmy Floyd Hasselbaink and Sabri Lamouchi. I loved playing on the beach: it's a goalkeeper's dream. When my dad came to pick me up at the end of the match, David shook his hand and said, 'Your son will go far.' I've met him since, and followed in his footsteps at Tottenham.

'GO FOR IT, IT'S ALL YOURS!'

Over the summer of 2005 Frédéric Antonetti was appointed Nice manager and I became a champion of Europe with the French under-19s in Belfast. Our team was an armada, as history would prove later, although I already had a feeling about it. There were several future French internationals (Yohan Cabaye, Abou Diaby, Younès Kaboul, Yoann Gourcuff and me), as well as many players who would go on to have great professional careers (Moussa Sow, Didier Digard, Yoan Gouffran, Geoffrey Jourdren, Djamel Abdoun, Florian Marange, Frédéric Sammaritano and Yassin Moutaouakil, who played several seasons in England). At that age, you meet foreign players you'll come across further down the line. In Belfast, I was mightily impressed by the German goalie, though I didn't catch his name. It was Manuel Neuer. He seemed to take up the entire goal, and when I saw him play with Schalke 04, a little later, I recognized him immediately.

The beginning of a professional career separates players who've grown up together. Up until then, you never know who will make it and who will be sidelined. This separation often depends on very little: bad luck, injury, a poor decision. I joined Nice's professional team in 2004, and signed my élite contract at the same time as three other young players – centre-forwards Kamel Larbi and Franck Padovani, and defender Anthony Scaramozzino – just after our under-18s French champions title. We'd beaten Lyon in the final, following a penalty shootout. We also had Rok Elsner with us, the younger brother of Luka, who would be my brother's manager at Le Havre. But out of this fine generation, I'm the only one who really made it at the top level, despite them all being immensely talented. Kamel Larbi went to Lorient on loan, but when he returned to Nice, things didn't go well with Fred Antonetti. Franck Padovani played four matches in Ligue 1 in 2005, before being loaned to Toulon then returning to the B team. Fabien Lamatina went off to play in Spain, Ismaël Gace made his career in Ligue 2, while Mathieu Pecastaing played several matches for Elche, in Spain, before becoming a pilot. There are always several ways to succeed.

Frédéric Antonetti's arrival shuffled the cards for everyone. I discovered a coach who made decisions according to merit, trusting the young'uns, but not hesitating to incentivize them too. Piling the pressure on in this way could work, given my volatile character on the pitch. I recall one day a couple of years earlier when I'd been asked to join a session with the pros to make the numbers up, and forward Malek Cherrad had called out mid-game, 'Hey, this isn't the World Cup, you know!' I can understand where he was coming from, but for me it *was* like the World Cup: I was 16 and, having come straight

'GO FOR IT, IT'S ALL YOURS!'

from a maths lesson to a practice session with the pros, I wasn't there just for fun. There's a side to me which is poised, discreet, respectful and rational; off the pitch, I would keep pretty quiet, you wouldn't have heard me pipe up. I wasn't changing in the pros' dressing room yet – I'd wait outside their door to be invited in. But on the pitch I didn't differentiate between a training session with guys of my age and one with the pros. I had the same energy and was really very aggressive.

I made my professional debut in a League Cup match against Châteauroux in autumn 2005. I am eternally grateful to Fred Antonetti, who straight away saw something in me, and yet was also able to incorporate me while preventing me from getting ahead of myself. I see him rarely these days, but I'm aware of how fundamental he was to my career. I owe him a lot. On the pitch, I no doubt performed adequately and repaid his trust, but he took the risk of playing a very young keeper, and that was rare at the time. Being quite reserved, we've never talked properly about those days, but I really appreciated him, and he was one of those managers whose sessions I preferred, even if we would start the week by running laps of the pitch. It wasn't a paternal relationship – I already had a dad – but our respective ages did come into it, and there was affection too. His assistant, Jean-Marie De Zerbi, was a peach. Bruno

Valencony became the goalie trainer, and though it was tough for him, since he would surely have wanted to play another year when they proposed this career change to him, he threw his weight into the mission to make me progress.

I was the number 2, but I was playing in the League Cup, and when we qualified for the final in spring 2006, Fred lined me up in Ligue 1 too by way of preparation, while also insisting that the club bosses give me a professional deal immediately, despite me still having an apprentice contract. I was starting to earn money, but I was only thinking of the present and my objectives. The cash from my first contracts went into an account I barely touched. I told myself that this was all so fragile and that I would need it later. Still, it enabled me to buy a car and to move into an apartment in the west of Nice (where Marine would often come to stay) in summer 2005, after returning from the under-19s European Championship, giving me greater independence – although this was relative given that the apartment was in the same complex as my parents'. I flew the family nest because my parents left early in the morning and got home late at night; but I went to see them after dinner sometimes, and I was at theirs every weekend.

The final of the League Cup was a superb experience, despite the 2–1 defeat to Nancy. I loved seeing so many Niçois in the Stade de France, and the whole city getting

'GO FOR IT, IT'S ALL YOURS!'

ready for the match for days. The loss remains a regret because it was the final, because it would have opened the doors of the UEFA Cup to us, and because it was my city, the place where I was born and grew up, not to mention that this was *my* club, the one with which I shared the rivalry with AS Monaco and AS Cannes. When I wore the Nice strip I always felt that it represented much more than a club to me. Even as a substitute, I was a true Niçois, and even when I was in the B team the Brigade Sud ultras would chant my name because I was the young Niçois who'd just won the under-18 French Championship and the under-19 European Championship. I could have started acting all boastful, but I've always been the type to keep my head down. I was aiming so high that I couldn't take myself for someone else when I hadn't done anything yet. When Marine and I went to do our shopping at the huge Cap 3000 mall, I would get asked for an autograph sometimes, but this early popularity was like water off a duck's back. Much had been made of me in the run-up to the League Cup final; I did my first TV appearances, for France 3 Provence-Alpes-Côte-d'Azur, and a segment in their *Tout le sport* show, if I recall correctly, as well as several interviews. It would be normal at that age to sit back and enjoy the modest cash and glimmers of fame. But I always had my sights set well ahead. I don't mean to suggest that I was mature, but I knew what I wanted: to succeed at Nice, then move on.

That League Cup final, which was my big première at the Stade de France – a stage I would return to so many times – is both a wonderful memory and a great disappointment. But I was young and part of me was thinking about my progression and becoming the team's number 1 keeper. That's how I've always functioned. Once I was the team's number 1, I would seek to become one of the best keepers in Ligue 1, and after that *the* best, and then the keeper for the French national team. I have always been obsessed by the next step. I didn't look beyond that, but I did look that far.

After the League Cup final, Damien Grégorini had ended the season as first-team keeper, and I remember my state of mind: I was polite, cordial and respectful, but I wanted to take his spot. I wasn't there to waste time, or apologize for myself. My idols were Fabien Barthez, Iker Casillas and Gigi Buffon, who all started very young, and if *they'd* not waited, there was no reason I should wait either. But talking the talk wasn't enough: I had to walk the walk, and so I played as if each practice session was a match to be won, live or die. I was already prepared to shoulder the responsibility, and my game showed this in spectacular fashion. When I think back to the risks I took – pushing the envelope, attempting to go after every ball in the penalty area, and constantly leaving the box too – I realize that I couldn't have played my whole career like that. Before each match, Grandpa would tell me, 'Don't forget, you're the boss.' Those words have stuck with me.

In the summer of 2006, three days before our away match in Le Mans, Fred Antonetti told me that I'd be OGC Nice's first-team keeper, at the age of 19. To be honest, although I did some really good things during the first ten matches, I had to adjust to the level in Ligue 1 as regards the speed of play and the density of players in the penalty area. I tried to maintain dominance but I felt there were things I needed to fix, such as the goal I let in at Le Mans, where I should have held back rather than rushing in to try to clear and getting beaten. But I made a mental note of everything: I took it all in, I learned my lessons, I got my hands on a lot of balls, and after those first ten matches I began helping my team to win points. We avoided relegation right at the end of the season, following a critical match away against Lyon in January 2007 (we drew 1–1) when the chairman, Maurice Cohen, was momentarily deposed by two shareholders. There was talk of Fred Antonetti being fired too, but they both stayed in the end, and this kicked off our rise up. That season, Lionel Letizi (who was trained at Nice), the former goalie for Metz, PSG and the French national team, arrived in January to guide me and help me reach my full potential. Also in January, we played Nantes away and Fabien Barthez made his debut in the Nantes strip. He had always been a model and an inspiration to me. When he shook my hand in the tunnel, I was like a kid. But beyond his reputation for being nice to other goalies, I felt something else too, a certain kindness. At the end of the match, which Nantes won 1–0, he came up to me on the pitch, hugged me round my neck, asked me for my shirt and said something to me that I've never forgotten: 'Go for it, it's all yours!' Whether this was a prediction or simply encouragement, I'm not sure, but I've still got his shirt, at my grandma's. Sure, it's an FC Nantes shirt, but it's Fabien's, that's what counts. Since then, he's told me that he'd like to give me a 'real shirt'. I'm waiting for it, Fabien; I've kept a space for it.

But January 2007 was also a very painful month because I lost my grandpa, the man who took me to practice, to matches, and who was always behind me. He'd had serious kidney problems and had been getting weaker as the months went by. He came to see me at practice less, but my grandparents' apartment remained the strategic bolthole it had always been throughout my years as a high school student and young pro footballer. Even once I was on the Nice roster, I ate lunch at theirs every day after practice; and

'GO FOR IT, IT'S ALL YOURS!'

before I got my driving licence, Grandma would drive me home, sometimes after a nap. They were there when I won the Toulon Tournament with the France under-21 team, after stopping a decisive penalty, and I gave Grandpa the best-goalkeeper trophy.

Since becoming the first-team keeper at Nice, Grandpa could only see me on the telly; and even though he was still with us for Christmas, he was very weak and he no longer left the house. I'm glad that I was able to tell him goodbye, and I hope that he recognized me that day, shortly before he died. At the training session following his death, I was so unable to focus that I went to see Jean-Marie De Zerbi, Fred Antonetti's assistant, to apologize and explain the reason why, having not said anything about it before because I kept everything to myself back then and didn't talk much.

Even though Grandpa was less present and didn't pressure me so much when I made my entry into the professional game, we still talked football together. He gave me a lot, and his death affected me deeply. You're never prepared when it happens. It was one more sign that my childhood was over. By way of honouring him and paying homage to everything he'd done and everything he'd been for me, I would become even better on the pitch. I owed it to him to progress further. He'd pushed me so far that I couldn't stop just because he was no longer there.

From then on, I really felt as if I was taking off. There was only one match, late on in the season, which went badly. I was at the end of my one-year contract, everyone was talking about me and I had contacts with other clubs. Away against Marseille, Pancho Abardonado and I bungled our communication on a long ball and Mamadou Niang scored. We lost 3–0 and at half-time Fred bawled us out: 'Yeah, that's what happens when you fail to focus on the everyday at the end of the season because you're already thinking of your next step!' I assumed he meant me, that I was thinking about leaving, which wasn't the case. In fact, when it came to the decisive matches following that one, he said nothing. I made some fantastic saves against Sedan, Valenciennes and PSG, which saved us from the drop. I was insane, taking massive risks, and it worked.

With my contract up, I was sitting on my apartment terrace one fine day in May when Fred rang. 'Coach,' I said, 'if you stay, I'll stay. I don't trust the club after what happened in Lyon in January, but I don't want to leave Nice, and I want to continue my development.' I signed a new contract with Nice, despite inducements from elsewhere. Before the end of the championship – and this was perhaps what Fred had been referring to after the Marseille game – I had met Gervais Martel, the chairman of Lens. And an Italian agent had set up an introduction with Inter, who

'GO FOR IT, IT'S ALL YOURS!'

had the Brazilian goalie Júlio César and wanted me as a long-term investment, even if it meant putting me out on loan. It was also around this time that I met Claudio Lotito, the Lazio boss, with whom I would talk again in summer 2023. I wanted to find out as much as I could about my options, and then decide. But deep down, I didn't want to leave. We had a great team and the next season would be much better. I would only have one break for injury, when I hurt my knee, made worse by resuming training again too vigorously and too soon. I took advantage of my recovery time to strengthen myself muscularly (resulting in a five-to-ten-metre gain on goalkicks), even though I stayed quite rangy. My oversized shirt and somewhat crazy playing style masked the fact that I was just skin and bones – 1.88 metres (6 foot 2 inches) yet just 74 kilogrammes. (It was at Lyon that I'd reach 78 kilogrammes, eventually weighing in at 84 kilogrammes in the latter part of my career.) The vogue for skin-tight jerseys in football did well to wait until I could fill them.

VI

A Star in the Sky Over Nice

My last season at Nice was one of sadness, grief and brotherhood.

My mother passed away one Thursday in April 2008. She'd had breast cancer once already, beating it after two or three years of treatment and struggle. Once in remission, she possibly hadn't kept enough of an eye on it and the disease spread to her gallbladder. Her health started to go downhill over Christmas and the first few weeks of 2008, but I told myself that since she'd already beaten cancer once, she'd beat it a second time. She never showed her discomfort or complained. When she left for the Princess Grace Hospital in Monaco for the last time, taking her laptop with her to continue working on her legal files, neither she, nor my father, nor us, the children, knew she wouldn't be coming home.

A STAR IN THE SKY OVER NICE

In her final few days she looked drawn and frail and spent a lot of time resting and sleeping. But when she was up to it, she continued to work. The day before she died, I had a funny feeling, I don't know why, but I took my brother, my grandma and Marine to see her. She was extremely weak. I remember giving her a little water, and I think that was the moment I realized. The next day, after training, I went back to my grandma's for lunch, and when I asked her, as soon as I got in the door, if she'd had any news of Mum from Dad, she answered that Mum had gone during the night. My dad had let me sleep then go to practice. We never hid things from each other, but he'd always sought to protect me. It was a hard and heavy thing to announce. Gautier was only 11 and dad wanted to shield him, even if it was tough, surely impossible. I went off to get some alone time. The next day, Friday, I told everyone and I went to train anyway. Fred Antonetti told me, 'You can give the match a miss, stay with your family.' But I decided to play. I simply asked for permission to eat with my family on Friday night before going to join the team on Saturday morning. I spent the evening with my father, my brother and my grandma, weighed down by grief that was hard to bear. But my father eventually turned to me and said, 'You've got a match to prepare for. Go to the hotel and get a good night's sleep.' I went to the Servotel, a ten-minute walk from the current stadium, and as I walked into the lobby, the coach and the staff were there to greet me. They had difficulty finding the words, but there wasn't much they could say; they were there and that's what mattered. The next day, I tried to prepare for the match as usual, knowing that it was impossible to do so, but when the club's long-time physio, Philippe Boulon, massaged me before the match, I felt as if he'd wrapped me in the warmth I needed.

The Stade du Ray observed a minute's silence for my mother before kick-off. It was quite something to share my grief with the city and my teammates. There's nothing like a team. I was 21 and going through a terrible family event, but I had such a warm, brotherly relationship with veterans like Lilian Laslandes, Cyril Rool and Olivier Echouafni that I felt protected and sheltered. They didn't leave me alone with my pain. I played a storming match against Lille. During the minute's silence, I had tried to control my emotion, but I had some bad energy to expel that night and it could only be done through physical effort. I was so very sad just before the match, and I was again as soon as it ended, and for a long time after that, but this game amid people who were there for me and wanted to protect me, proved a sort of escape from the sadness. If I'd had to play for myself, I would have fallen apart. It was because I owed it to the others that I was able to play a real match under such circumstances. I had, unfortunately, gone through this pain a year earlier, after the death of my grandpa, and had buried myself in work: I wanted to continue to make him proud. I felt the same excessively intense and sometimes contradictory emotions that evening, but I knew that I wanted to play well for Mum, too. A few days later, the whole team attended the funeral, which took place in Carras, close to where I lived, and after the service the players formed a guard of honour outside with the rest of the club. They'll always be the guys who were there for me. This awful event also showed the beauty of sport, the solidarity and the kindness.

I remember my father's dignity throughout, how reserved he was. He shielded us completely and, as he tried to sort everything out – the service, the burial – my grandma looked after us. As regards our mother's illness, he took the attitude that he was protecting us by not telling us everything. We knew some of it, but not everything, and it's often that way in the family: some things are a little hazy and you have to suss them out. But we got through it, and my father has become more open with the passing years and life's challenges; now that Gautier and me are grown up it's easier to discuss things with him. But he wanted to shield us back then, and so did Mum, whom I never heard complain.

These ordeals made me a little robotic. I kept all the feelings inside; I didn't want to express my sadness. I took refuge in work and competition – that's how I protected myself. I didn't want grief to eat away at me. I'm sensitive, though, but I tried not to show it. Marine remembers that I was a sad chap at home, but I found my escape in footie, where I tried to forget. Our family has always been very reserved: never any great demonstrations of joy, little in the way of great sadness. We don't let anyone in, we internalize things and we keep them to ourselves. Football was my release; it was my way of mourning.

Leaving my Nice cocoon to go to Lyon in the summer of 2008 took me out of my sadness somewhat, but I would have also liked to continue sharing that sadness with my family and my brother. I put myself in Gautier's place. He would have to go through his entire schooldays without our mum. Fortunately, we could always count on Grandma. She remains the rock of the family. We don't talk much, but we have always confided in her and, when possible, continue to go and have lunch at this great cook's, who has played tennis her whole life at the Monte-Carlo Country Club – the most beautiful courts in the world. She obviously became a maternal figure for Gautier. When I stopped by Nice recently, my father told me that Gautier calls Grandma every Friday. We each have our own habits with her.

A STAR IN THE SKY OVER NICE

I had ups and downs, of course, particularly since I tended to keep everything bottled up back then. I had already reacted in the same way to Grandpa's death. Never a chatterbox, I've become a bit more loquacious with age, with life, and experience, but back then nothing would come out. I know it wasn't easy for Marine to see me repress everything because she'd gone through the whole thing with us too. When she finished classes early at the university, she'd pop in to see my mum and take care of her, heat up some food for her or simply make sure she was OK.

I felt it was time to leave Nice and move on to the next stage of my career, but my mother's death held me back. I told myself that if I stayed another year, I could be with my dad and my little brother. My sister was in a different phase of her life, having lived in Paris for some years already, and although she was still very much there for us, I wouldn't be leaving her behind if I decided to move on. We talked about it together at the end of the season, and Gautier, who wanted me to succeed, urged me to leave. He was only 12.

In June 2008 I met several clubs. Tottenham first, by way of an interview in Paris with Damien Comolli (then director of football) and Juande Ramos (the manager at the time). Next was AC Milan, a club I'd always dreamed about. Željko Kalac was playing, but Dida had some serious back problems and Christian Abbiati was on loan to Atlético Madrid. So I talked with the two Milanese big cheeses, Adriano Galliani and Ariedo Braida. While there, I even ran into Yoann Gourcuff and his father, who were in talks about loaning Yo out to Bordeaux. We all had lunch together: my dad, me, Yoann, his dad, Galliani and Braida. Following initial discussions that morning, the serious business began in the afternoon. Once upstairs, instead of entering Galliani's office, Braida and Galliani took me into the trophy room and asked, 'Is there a player you really like?' 'Kaka,' I answered, and they immediately brought me his shirt. Milan gave me a real buzz.

Not long after, I was told that Lyon were interested, but I had yet to meet anyone when my dad called me to say that he was at the OGC Nice offices with Marino Faccioli, the administrative director of Olympique Lyonnais (OL), Rémi Garde, the scouting director, and Maurice Cohen, my chairman. 'Drop by the club,' he told me. I listened to what they had to say, Lyon being the biggest French club of those past few years, having just won seven French Championship titles in a row. They explained that Grégory Coupet was going to leave. Next I got a call from OL's goalie coach, Joël Bats, *the* keeper from the Platini generation, a European champion in 1984. He called me a second time, then a third. As goalie coach he had been involved in Bernard Lama's

A STAR IN THE SKY OVER NICE

success at PSG and Greg Coupet's at OL. He knew how to talk to me: 'Come work with me, Hugo, the sky's the limit for us.' I sensed that he was sincere and genuine, as I would have the opportunity to confirm. Even Greg Coupet called me to clarify his personal situation, as well as to praise both the club and Joël, assuring me that this transfer could be a really important step in my development.

So I had three propositions: Lyon, Tottenham and Milan. As much as Milan made me dream, I signed for OL. In Joël, I found a paternal figure who took me under his wing. I was still a little young, with oodles of ambition, but lots of respect too, and I realized that this was a big club which believed in me and was prepared to send me out onto the great battlefield that was the Champions League. I also knew that it was a good path to the French national team.

I was 21, which was young to be the incumbent keeper at such a club. It was also the first time I'd moved away from Nice. My dad, my brother and my grandma all told me the same thing: 'Go for it. It'll make all the effort you've put in worth it; and you'll come see us often.' The hardest thing, without a doubt, was leaving my baby brother behind at a time like that. It also meant new beginnings for Marine, who managed to sort herself out a place at Lyon Uni all on her own to do the second year of her Master's degree in human resources management and law, after having passed the first year of her Master's in social psychology at Nice. We'd met in the last year of high school and had started going out six months after final exams, so moving to Lyon was a new adventure for us both, and one which would further cement our relationship. She was a reassuring presence in such a painful period for our family – at least I would have some stability somewhere. She wasn't a football fan at first, but she lived it through me, and I don't think I can have been that easy to live with. In fact, I know I wasn't, because I simply couldn't stand losing. Also, I didn't speak much at the start of the relationship, I was very introverted. I started to express myself with time. I only have lovely things to say about our relationship, what we've built together, our children, the mother she is to them: fiercely protective – a proper woman of the South (what with her Italian roots). She had to adapt to the rhythm of matches and my travelling. After Anna-Rose was born, Marine often found herself alone in Lyon – at 24 years old that can't always have been easy for her. Luckily, her aunt lived in Villefranche-sur-Saône, 30 kilometres or so north of Lyon, not far from our bolthole in the village of Limonest, and she often spent the weekend with her, amid the Beaujolais vineyards. We loved Lyon. It's where we became adults.

VII

Final Four

Olympique Lyonnais dominated French football, but this ambitious and highly financially structured club placed a premium on interpersonal relations, at the direction of Jean-Michel Aulas, a chairman who was very close to the players. When I signed with Lyon they were between managers, but I'd been confidentially informed of the imminent arrival of Claude Puel. The day of my signing, I finally had a chat with Joël Bats as I crossed the street from the club's headquarters with Jean-Michel Aulas, his special advisor Bernard Lacombe, my dad, Nice chairman Maurice Cohen and Marino Faccioli, to have lunch at Argenson, just behind the Gerland stadium. I sensed that Joël was happy to be starting something with me; we shared a desire to write our own story and he straight away pegged me for the young man and young keeper that I was. I gave him my trust, did everything he asked of me, and he taught me how to play at the highest level, as well as telling me what I might expect as my career progressed. It was the start of a long, firm friendship, and we are still very much in touch. Meeting him was one of the most important events in my life. He called me 'Poulet' (a term of endearment in French), as he did all his goalies.

On my best behaviour, I tiptoed into a dressing room that had won the last seven French championships with such stars as Juninho, Cris, Sidney Govou, the rising talent Karim Benzema, Fred, and all the internationals: Anthony Réveillère, Jean-Alain Boumsong and Jérémy Toulalan (a wonderful player and all-round great guy); not forgetting a World Cup winner, Fabio Grosso. I was also mightily impressed by the talent of Mathieu Bodmer, who was my football-tennis partner: you only had to loft him the ball and he would clinically finish the rally.

As a young talent signing for the best club in France and multiplying my salary, I might easily have been overwhelmed, but I had nothing but humility and respect, and in return everyone welcomed me with open arms. That's why I retain a particular affection for the club.

Everyone, from supporters to the club bosses to the municipality, did all they could to make me feel welcome. They adopted me immediately. In Nice, folks told me, 'People aren't nice in Lyon, and it's cold too, you'll see.' But I liked the people in Lyon, and in summer the city's an oven.

At the training camp in Tignes, Robert Duverne – the fitness coach of both OL and Les Bleus – really made me suffer. My body wasn't up to it; I didn't have the lungs. Joël made me work on this. I nearly threw up during our first windscreen-wiper sessions. With Claude Puel having arrived, there were sometimes three training sessions a day: jogging before breakfast; a gym session at 10 a.m.; and pitch practice in the afternoon. Truth be told, I wasn't ready. But Joël, who treated his goalies like Formula 1 drivers, always paying attention to the smallest detail, would prepare me to play match after match. I was raw material, a ball of energy; I didn't know how to pace myself, so I had to learn how to ease off two days before a match – maybe put my gloves down and do something else – then pick up again with some fast jogging the week after the match. In the run-up to games, Joël would tell me what the play would be like depending on the upcoming opponents: maybe a lot of aerial play, or deep balls. Joël was more than a goalie trainer: he had an overview of things, and it was he who put together the videos with Bruno Génésio, the assistant manager at the time. Claude Puel had brought Patrick Collot with him, and relations between the new pair and the longstanding staff were easier when we were winning.

FINAL FOUR

As far as the goalies were concerned, it was pretty clear to me that Rémy Vercoutre – Grégory Coupet's stand-in for some years – was rather disappointed not to be made number 1 keeper. He had played a lot the previous season, following Grégory Coupet's injury, and his reaction was to be expected. But during a team-bonding evening, when we'd had a few drinks after eating dinner together, Rémy put his arm round me and said that I was talented and that he'd back me all the way. From that moment on, I understood what kind of man he was, and I knew that he would always be positive. I think, too, that he appreciated that a guy as quiet as me could be such a good party companion at such a late hour of the night. I really loved those moments, the virtues of which I'd discovered in Nice with the arrival of Lilian Laslandes who, apart from being a stupendous centre-forward (even at the age of 38), was a real people guy who liked staying out late sometimes and who helped us get through some difficult periods by getting us all to socialize together once a month, allowing us to get to know each other better outside of footie. Rémy was cut from the same cloth. He had a candid way and we got on well.

When I arrived in Lyon they told me about two things: the derby against AS Saint-Étienne – the reason why we should never wear green while travelling to training, or even around town – and the Champions League. The 2008 season began with us losing the Trophée des Champions (an annual super cup contested between the champions of Ligue 1 and the winners of the Coupe de France) away to Bordeaux following a penalty shootout, despite me having saved the first two. In the autumn, we were favourites for the title, having had a seven-point lead over Bordeaux, but we slumped in the spring, losing our leading position and finishing in a tricky spot. I had discovered the resilience and the weight of the dressing room of a major team – as well as its tribal groupings. It was said that the players and the rest of the staff had sidelined the previous manager, Alain Perrin; clearly the club had appointed Claude Puel in order to be done with such antics, and this was also what made our season so complicated. Tensions would reveal themselves in January in a clash between Fred – our Brazilian centre-forward – and the coach in relation to a video. Fred's name came up a lot in the post-match analysis from the coaching staff, and he stood up suddenly and shouted, 'Fred, Fred, always Fred!' then left yelling in Portuguese. Relations between Puel and Juninho, as well as other leading players such as Sidney Govou and Cris, also became tense. Even though I was concentrating on my challenge to succeed Greg Coupet, it was all too clear to me that we were playing badly, or not as the players

FINAL FOUR

would like, and that we depended far too much on Karim Benzema.

That season, I discovered the Champions League: the music, the stars on the shirts and the stars in the eyes; the major teams, the weeks with two matches. It began for me with a 1-1 draw against Bayern, followed by a somewhat mixed match away to Bucharest, which I didn't like at all, but was fortunately without consequence – we won it 3-5. We still held out hope up until the round of 16 against Barcelona. After a 1-1 draw at home, a real storm broke over Camp Nou for the away leg, and after being 4-0 down in the first half (conceding four goals in 17 minutes), we clawed our way back to 4-2; Karim had a shot at making it 4-3, but it went flying over the crossbar. Final score: 5-2. Barcelona were simply unplayable that season.

Lyon also saw the start of my successive throat infections. They were awful, occurred three or four times a year and were accompanied by a raging fever. Maybe the fact that we were playing matches every three days – a new rhythm for me – had something to do with it; the fatigue must have worn down my immune system, and no doubt I wasn't eating enough between games to keep my strength up either. They lasted throughout my entire time at OL. Sometimes I played with a fever, and even when we managed to bring it down, I remained off-colour and achy, although the adrenaline and my strong mindset carried me through, enabling me to focus on the match and throw myself into the arena without thinking about it. For six years, these afflictions went on. Six years of wearing a scarf, drying my hair and wearing a beanie. Bizarrely, they disappeared after two seasons at Tottenham.

Spring 2009 was Bordeaux's crowning glory. The quality of their play was remarkable during those years. We finished third, overwhelmed by the disappointment of our seven-year reign as French champions slipping away. I hadn't seen it coming. We'd been the leaders for a long time, but the problems were there: Juni was set to leave, Karim too; we felt the wheels coming off, and the final sprint revealed our fragility. We also felt the opposing forces of change and stability in the club, and a mutual incomprehension: Claude Puel had come to build something, but in a club which had dominated French football to such an extent, there was nothing new to build.

We weren't French champions in 2009. Or 2010. Or 2011. Or 2012. I have never been French champion. But in Lyon, I became another player and another man, experiencing great seasons and amazing moments, such as in spring 2010, when I played in the semi-finals of the Champions League, a participant in one of those huge matches which had made me dream as a kid in front of my grandparents' telly.

FINAL FOUR

In summer 2009 OL bought Lisandro López (soon nicknamed Licha), Aly Cissokho, Michel Bastos and Bafé Gomis, a real classy guy. Everyone was very quickly in agreement about Licha's talent on the pitch and his grit.

We were leaders of the championship after eight days, but there was so much change in the team that the continuity had disappeared. I don't know if rebuilding the team was really the correct thing to do, or whether it would have been better to rely on the experience within it. I had the impression that experience was less of a factor after the departure of Juni and Karim, in spite of the presence of several longstanding players such as Anthony Réveillère, Cris, Sidney Govou and Kim Källström. But we should have been champions, all the same. As for me, I was suffering from a sports hernia, which was treated at length by the club's veteran physios, Patrick Perret and Abdel Redissi – two exceptional people on both a professional and a human level.

Luckily, we did experience some fabulous moments in the Champions League, such as my first visit to Anfield in the group stage where we beat Liverpool 1–2. Jérémy Toulalan had to switch to centre-back after Cris's injury, the young Max Gonalons equalized and Chelito Delgado scored the winning goal in extra time.

Throughout the years when OL dominated French football, the club played regularly in the Champions League, yet never managed to pull something out of the hat in the knockout stages, getting through the first knockout round three times (against Real Sociedad, PSV Eindhoven and Werder Bremen), but failing to progress beyond the quarter-finals. So it was as we lined up against a Real Madrid containing Ronaldo, Benzema, Kaká, Higuaín, Casillas and Ramos in February 2010. Following our first-leg victory (1–0) from a goal by Jean II Makoun, the second-leg match at the Bernabéu has gone down in the club's history. Ronaldo scored very early on – a frustrating goal because the ball, a blistering strike, passed straight between my legs. I made several major saves after that and, in the second half, we were wonderfully cohesive and tough until Miré Pjanic (a huge talent) scored to take us through to the quarter-finals (1–1). It's impossible to forget your first time at the Bernabéu. The place pulses with history. It was a huge pleasure to discover it and to qualify on its turf. This was also the first time I met Iker Casillas, whom I greeted with a feeling of both admiration and rivalry. I wanted to tell him that he was an amazing goalie, that I had a vast amount of respect for him and that he had inspired me in my youth – but that I was determined to beat him. This was also the night that Licha posted a message on the flipchart in the dressing room before the match. He'd called Cris the day before to translate it into French, but Rémy Vercoutre did the honours in the end: 'Tonight it's until death do us part. We can't leave this stadium without having given our all. Let's make sure we have no regrets. Good luck everyone, Licha.' He needed to express himself and, not speaking enough French to make a speech just before the match, wanted to convey a message to us that was short and to the point, to create a different mood in the dressing room before our biggest game of the season. None of us forgot this message, which was essentially the same as the one he always communicated on the pitch, where he was an amazing leader, urging us on. We would follow him gladly.

Off the pitch, Licha was a chap who liked a peaceful life. He became my neighbour when he got a place in the same residential complex as me in Limonest, north of Lyon, which of course brought us closer in friendship. We would share a *maté* before heading off to training together, and we also spent time with Sidney Govou and Rémy Vercoutre. Rémy spoke a little Spanish, so he acted as a kind of a bridge, but I don't really know how we all managed to chat together. Still, Licha picked up a fair bit of French quite fast. He was clever and sometimes all we needed to communicate was a look, the natural language of two shy guys. We hung out a lot, and I missed our rituals when I left Lyon in 2012.

That summer, when Marine was in Nice, I ate at Licha's place all the time; we were watching a Racing Club de Avellaneda match when Tottenham's offer arrived, and he told me to go for it. Racing Club was his home team, from back in Buenos Aires, and we would often take in games together, at all hours.

After eliminating Real we had to play Bordeaux in the quarter-finals of the Champions League. It was weird to face off against another French team, but it's a cherished memory, particularly since I was on fire for both the home and away legs. We played the first leg at Gerland, where we did quite well and punished Bordeaux for their errors. But despite our 3–1 win we knew that the second leg would be a real slog. Licha didn't play (a suspension), we conceded a goal just before half-time, and the end of the match was a whirlwind, with ball after ball entering our penalty area until I made a decisive save from a Wendel header (one of my top five, but more on that later). Still, we'd hung on (0–1) and it was magnificent. For the first time, the club was in the semi-finals of the Champions League, the final four of the most prestigious club competition in the world.

We will never know what might have been had Eyjafjallajökull not erupted in Iceland, sending a cloud of volcanic ash drifting across Europe and grounding air traffic to an unprecedented extent. Having flown to Bordeaux, we had to return by coach, then cram into a minibus to Munich for the first leg of our Champions League semi-final, the biggest match in the history of OL (and in most of our careers at that point). The journey took eight hours, not counting the stops to stretch our legs. It was hardly the best preparation for such a high-profile game and did little to help our recovery in the busiest period of the season. The match started well, with Bayern reduced to ten men after Franck Ribéry's red card. But in the second half, Jérémy Toulalan was sent off in turn and Arjen Robben scored in the 69th minute. The floating strike had been masked from me by Max Gonalons as he turned away from it, so delaying my reaction time. Scorers remember all their goals; keepers too.

Down 1–0, we might have dreamed of pulling off something special in the home leg at Gerland, but not for long. We probably attacked too hard, too fast, after the head coach's rousing words on the need to score straight away, when he could have asked us to be more calculating and ensure some kind of equilibrium instead of opening ourselves up and getting shot to pieces. 'A Spanking from Olić' screamed the press after the Bayern striker Ivica Olić scored a hat-trick in a 3–0 win. We felt like we'd been steamrollered. But as Champions League semi-finalists and Ligue 1 runners-up, it was hardly a washout season. I was in the right place, I told myself. I still didn't have any silverware, but I sensed that there was a collective progression alongside my own personal evolution – for I had become the tenured keeper of the French national team, and my sights were firmly set on my first World Cup, in South Africa. It was a huge opportunity to make history. I could never have guessed the manner in which we would do so . . .

VIII

A Proper Playoff

When I signed with Lyon, the club which represented France in the Champions League and showcased its players most prominently, I was clearly thinking about the French national team. I didn't have to wait long. My first call-up came in August 2008 in Sweden (we won 2–3), where Steve Mandanda would be number 1 keeper. Although Raymond Domenech hadn't announced an official pecking order in the squad, I imagine that Steve knew he would be playing. I, however, didn't know that I would not. I have never thought of myself as a substitute and I have never accepted being one; I've always had the ambition to be more. Steve had the standing and the talent, and had been at Euro 2008, two months earlier. So I remained myself – discreet, courteous, proper and very respectful of Steve, whom I'd already rubbed shoulders with in the under-21s – but there was no question of me accepting the role of sub.

A PROPER PLAYOFF

Steve was coming out of a superb season with Olympique de Marseille (OM), carving out a place for himself in the most popular club in France, but this only motivated me more. I had no wish to wait, yet I was benched once, twice, four times, until I told myself in October that I would at least play the friendly against Tunisia and celebrate my first selection. Instead of which, I was sent to play in the second leg of France's under-21s qualifier against Germany, in Metz. France under-21s was a team I had moved on from and whose goalie, Rémy Riou, had performed effectively in their first leg. I played a decent match in Metz, but we were eliminated by a last-minute goal. The whole thing was disrespectful to Riou and to the notion of a group pursuing a joint objective. I took it very badly, it's true: either I was part of the deal, playing both the first and second legs in a collective week-long adventure, or else don't pick me at all. Showing up for 48 hours, that wasn't nice, and it wasn't proper as regards the two keepers, Rémy Riou and Benoît Costil – at least not according to my notions of how to manage a squad.

  I would be rewarded with my first selection a month later, against Uruguay, perhaps because Les Bleus had had some bumps since the summer and this friendly was a good opportunity to see me at work. If you're picked for the national team, you have to know how to seize your chance at the right moment. It was the start of a long goalie duel, since we were high performers at our clubs, but I didn't yet feel the pressure, in November 2008. My first international game was very intense. We'd started out from the Clairefontaine national football training centre on match day. The journey was long and the match was a blur of excitement, as well as pride on behalf of my family, who were watching on the telly. My late mum and grandpa were ever-present in my thoughts. That first cap gave meaning to everything that I had done up until that point, all of the choices and all of the sacrifices. I stepped out onto the grass of the Stade de France behind Patrick Vieira and in front of Thierry Henry.

For me, that first cap was just one more stage in my progression. I already wanted more. This wasn't the first time that I had been picked after being number 2. That had already happened to me in the under-14s in Ligue Méditerranée under Bruno Bini, the future manager of the French women's team: I had sat on the bench watching the tenured keeper play less well than me, and after two defeats I finally played in the third match, which we won after a penalty shootout. In the under-18s I had to wait again, before leapfrogging Geoffrey Jourdren. I always had to go out and hunt down my number 1 spot; I've never been handed anything. Not that I'm complaining; ever since the youth teams in Nice, I've fed off the rivalries to become the best. Even upon signing with Tottenham in 2012, when I was already the keeper of the French team, I had to earn my place as the incumbent keeper. Only Olympique Lyonnais trusted me with the role straight away, which is why I maintain such links with the club and gratitude to it.

It was a while before I played for Les Bleus again, but there were no issues between Steve and me. Bruno Martini, the goalie coach, protected us equally; and the staff included Fabrice Grange, who'd been there during the tricky coexistence of Fabien Barthez and Grégory Coupet in 2006, when they had to have separate goalkeeping coaches. With Steve there was never any tension, but buckets of mutual respect. The tensions would come later, but not between him and me, neither in practice nor within the day-to-day of the team. They would come from outside, in the inevitable staging of a rivalry by the media.

I wouldn't play an international again until France played Turkey (1-0) in a friendly in June 2009, at home at Gerland, in front of my dad for the first time. The atmosphere was crazy, with thousands of Turkish supporters throwing full bottles of Coke at me. It remained to be seen which of Steve and me would be titular keeper to kick off the next season, starting in August. I knew it would be me the day before the match in the Faroe Islands, during practice, when Raymond

Domenech approached me. We won 0–1 in the wind and the rain, and in September I played our next match, against Romania, followed by my sending-off in Serbia after only nine minutes, accused of a foul on Nikola Žigic, which VAR would surely have overturned. I was worried about my future with Les Bleus. My dad swears I even shouted to him, 'It's over for me in the French team!' as I walked back to the dressing room. Steve came on in my place, did everything he had to do, while I was in a deep dark hole because of the red card and the feeling of injustice. I recall Titi (Thierry Henry), who had equalized, saying to Nicolas Anelka after the game, 'Nico, do you realize what it means, this figure of 50 goals?' He was proud, and quite right too. He would score one more goal before the end of his international career.

Back in Lyon, my doubts faded and my performance levels with OL remained high. Raymond Domenech would start me against Austria in October, even though my hernia had flared up, with stabbing pain. But I wanted to play, no matter what. The World Cup playoffs against Ireland were a month later, but a series of intense and somewhat insane events in the days preceding the matches did nothing to dampen talk of a rivalry with Steve.

One Sunday evening at Gerland, a few days before the first leg, came the famous 5–5 draw between Lyon and Mar-

A PROPER PLAYOFF

seille, played as debate swirled around the two top French goalies. I made at least one error: on the first goal, trying to catch a vaguely floating strike from Benoît Cheyrou that I should have punched away. On the second, again I could have done better, even though I was very unlucky how it played out: I'd pushed the ball towards my post, and it struck the post again before entering the goal. It was a below-par performance – which I would have stomached better if we'd won 5–4 – and a far from successful match for either me or Steve. Arriving at Clairefontaine the next day for the prep before our two playoff matches against Ireland, nobody knew who would be the number 1 goalkeeper. Even though I'd been playing since the summer and had got my place back after the red-card suspension, Raymond had never announced it. But deep down, the situation suited my psychology, for I never told myself that I *was* number 1 or number 2, only that I had to *become* number 1; that I wanted to play and that I had to go out and hunt down my place. I was competing only against myself. Had I fixated on Steve, it would not have augured well.

I was picked to play, following another joint training session with Fabien Barthez – an idea of Raymond's to better nurture two young goalkeepers. I've always appreciated Fabien's talent and character. Very early on, he said in an interview that he really liked what 'little Lloris at Nice' was doing. He always supported me, yet without ever taking sides for Steve or for me.

These two playoff matches to qualify for that troubled World Cup in South Africa hold a particular place in my career and in my memories. Not only because they were major matches for Les Bleus and for me (I was only 22), but also because the media wondered if I deserved to be the number 1 keeper, especially after the Ireland manager, Giovanni Trapattoni, had declared the day before the match that I was one of France's weak points. My grandma kept the press cuttings, all the headlines on the saviour, the hero, the man of the match, two 8 out of 10s in *L'Équipe* and, after the first leg, 'France Has its Goalie', 'A Perfect Leap' and 'Lloris Makes History for Les Bleus'; then, following the second leg, 'He Kept Them Alive', 'Thanks Again, Lloris!' and 'Lloris, the Lone Hero'. I'm not saying I was unaware of what they were saying or writing about me at the time, but it's now that I appreciate it, just like I can finally appreciate the entirety of my career. I said in an interview that I'd only been doing my job. It wasn't the whole truth. I was proud of having been on top of my game; proud of my performances.

We won 0-1 in Dublin (the goal from Nico Anelka), and even though I'd been told that the aerial balls would be truly punishing, it was those where I was most effective. I

A PROPER PLAYOFF

can hear Bruno Martini saying after the match, 'It's huge what you did today, Hugo.' But I didn't realize it, and was already thinking about the second leg. Perhaps I'd surprised many people, but not me. I'd already fought similar battles in other situations. That first leg of the playoff was a pivotal game, watched by 12 million TV viewers, in the unbelievable arena of Croke Park, filled with 90,000 fans, and the Irish national anthem belted out just before kick-off with a fervour to wake the dead. I had never seen such a huge stadium. I loved the passion and the hostility, they supercharged me. I knew that all eyes were on me, and not just because of Trapattoni's 'weak point' comment. The match was a real battle and there were no easy saves. The first one sent me diving to Robbie Keane's feet to gather the ball, in that very dynamic, almost extreme style I had at the time in duels, always going forward. The second was on an aerial ball in the second half, the subject of a wonderful photograph of me soaring above Kevin Doyle.

Everyone remembers the second leg playoff at the Stade de France. The Irish were 0–1 up pretty quickly, but that didn't bother me particularly. I felt in sound shape, heading out to snatch all the aerial balls, sometimes far from my goal; and even when the Irish goalie Shay Given came up for the last corner, when we were 1–1 and already had our qualification for the World Cup in the bag, I came out to intercept and block the ball. We didn't control much in that return match, it's true – we were gripped by the fear of losing it all and the fans were spooked – but the jitteriness hadn't affected me. Those few days were a big step forward in my career in blue. From that moment on, people looked at me differently.

The match was so heated that, from my penalty area, I didn't see Thierry Henry's handball on William Gallas's equalizer in extra time. And I didn't comprehend the fallout from it. This playoff was a massive, uncertain struggle, but there wasn't a single minute in either of the two games when we risked elimination. When Thierry Henry controlled the ball with his hand, we were heading into a penalty shootout, maybe, but we weren't out of contention. I thought it terribly unfair the treatment meted out to Titi. I had the feeling he was being made to pay for something else. I didn't understand the debate in France: you really have to have zero sporting culture to want the match to be replayed, when such events lie at the very heart of the history and mythology of the game. Why was Maradona's handball the Hand of God and Titi's the Hand of the Devil, when both derived from exactly the same thing, a player's instinctive reflex?

Just after the match, and unaware of the coming media and political storm, Joël Bats surprised me in the corridor. I

A PROPER PLAYOFF

didn't know he was coming. We went back to Lyon together that night on the OL plane, and I gave him the yellow shirt I'd worn, which resembled the one he'd donned in the Platini years. He had been the goalie of the French team in the World Cup of 1986, the year I was born, and now I would be too. Seven months later, I would almost be reproached for having helped the French team to qualify.

IX

Knysna

The clouds appeared quite quickly. And, as much as 2010 had been shaping up to be a beautiful year – what with a Champions League semi-final for OL in the spring and my first World Cup – the sky remained overcast for the French national team. We lost 0–2 to Spain in March, weighed down by the controversies and the fever surrounding our return match against Ireland. The Spanish made us run after the ball, and when we had possession we didn't make the right choices. A negative atmosphere surrounded us, with French politicians leveraging our poor performance for their own purposes, not to mention demonstrating their lack of sporting culture. They reproached us for having cheated, despite that instance of handball being part of the game – you only have to have played footie in a school playground to realize this. With the exception of a few days – first at training camp in Tignes, then a pretty successful friendly against Costa Rica in Lens (2–1) – the tension remained high; everything was wonky, I see no other way to describe it.

After such a long time, it all tends to be reduced to the players' strike and a crisis of morale. But what happened in South Africa is more complex. There is one explanation for the strike and another for the failure. People forget that the failure came before the strike. That the responsibilities were shared. That we were alone, without high-level personnel around us. That the domestic atmosphere had been heavy since the autumn. That the manager was running out of steam – Laurent Blanc having already been named as his replacement – which took away a considerable chunk of Raymond Domenech's power in the eyes of the players, given the historic tensions half of them had with him. We were very nearly a team after Tignes, yet we failed. You can't tackle a World Cup without deep collective values, without each player wanting to fight for everyone else. But that's what we did, in the course of a training camp unworthy of a great footballing nation. It's where it all began and where it all ended.

At Tignes I believed in our renaissance for a few days, after the positive effect of a meeting called by Thierry Henry, who spoke of his incomprehension at the lack of clarity regarding the head coach's game-plans. For an hour, Henry called for specifics from the staff. Even at a time when he was in some difficulty at his club (he was hardly playing at Barcelona), Titi was thinking of the squad. We – or at least I – didn't yet know that the manager had been to see him in Barcelona to tell him that he wouldn't be going to the World Cup, before changing his mind when he got back. Now I think that the key players of the team must have known. The meeting in Tignes had a positive impact: the training sessions were really good, as were the non-footie activities, such as the night we spent in a high mountain hut, which would sadly bring Lassana Diarra's World Cup to an end before it began when he was struck down with altitude sickness. I arrived at Tignes by helicopter with the other Lyon players, to be greeted by the famous Niçois shepherd on his trusty bicycle. The guy had known me since childhood. He would watch the matches at the Stade du Ray perched in a tree in a corner, and could be found strolling about on winter evenings with his skis on his shoulder.

I don't know exactly why it all went off the rails. But I do know where and when: Tunisia, location of the second stage of our World Cup prep, where our families had joined us. There was a before and an after. I saw the change, suddenly, in the second preparation match, in Radès, against Tunisia: the positive energy, the sense of a rebirth, the promises, the collective spirit, it had all gone. I've been told a few times that it was the Zahia affair – a sex scandal involving certain members of Les Bleus (at least according to the media) – which had spoiled the atmosphere when the wives and partners arrived. But it was above all the issue of the captaincy, which was assigned to Patrice Evra, something that William Gallas couldn't swallow. I was just a kid, 23 years old, so I wasn't asked to pick sides, but I felt the tension. After Tunisia, relations in the squad would never be the same.

The truth, too, was that the French Football Federation made a real hash of things. We did the preparation camps to make them happy, with a stop in Tunisia and another on the island of La Réunion, where the weather was poor and the pitches hazardous. I experienced later World Cups where nothing was left to chance. Not this one. The start of my adventure was also the end of an era.

La Réunion was clearly a step too far, with a 1–0 defeat to the Chinese third team on an atrocious pitch. The whole episode only served to cruelly expose the problems that would overwhelm us: the isolation of Raymond Domenech, who no longer had the support of the team stalwarts; the hazy play; the lack of a cohesive team spirit; the crystallization of various tensions surrounding the media focus on and popularity of Yoann Gourcuff; and the frustrations of William Gallas, who had a dodgy calf and still hadn't got over the whole captaincy thing. He just wasn't the same. His disappointment was visible and intrusive. He'd received the news quite unceremoniously, in the dressing room in Lens in front of everyone else before the match against Costa Rica, and the manner in which he'd been told only added to his sense of hurt.

Stepping onto South African soil, our collective baggage had simply become too cumbersome. Still, I was all starry-eyed, this being my first World Cup. Whatever the general feeling, I was personally filled with a mix of excitement, expectation and hope. And in the team, amid the strains and the doubts, you could feel what this tournament meant to so many players with African roots. But there was always a 'but', a glitch, a shadow. And our arrival at the base camp left us circumspect. I remember our first impression upon discovering the super-luxury Pezula Hotel in Knysna, overlooking the ocean: 'What on earth are we doing here, at the world's end, far from everything?' The nearest airport was a two-hour drive away, and the training pitch was a disgrace. The hotel itself was exceptional, but the pitch was in a basin, and since it was autumn, it rained a lot. Of all the hotels I've stayed in with the French team, this was the most luxurious, but I don't know if it was appropriate. In the final stage of a tournament, you do need to be somewhat isolated to focus on your goals, but a player also needs to feel something of everyday life and the country they're in, the outside pressure too. At Pezula the excessive isolation played its part in the catastrophe and the awful succession of events.

As we kicked off the competition, playing Uruguay (0-0) in Cape Town, the whole squad was all in, even William. We had discovered this magnificent city the day before: Table Mountain above us, the ocean right next to the stadium. We'd watched the opening match on telly, as well as the Shakira concert the day before that. Finally, we felt the power of the event. The next day, we played a good match against Uruguay, creating the best opportunities, including one by Sidney in the first half. Their goalie, Fernando Muslera, was of my generation; we would cross paths many times. At future press conferences before big competitions, I would often emphasize how important the first match is. You weaken yourselves if you don't win it because the second match instantly becomes a final, since you're virtually eliminated if you lose it. With this 0-0 draw we were disappointed, but it wasn't a crisis. We remained in the competition, with our problems, our collective liabilities, our imperfect play, but qualifiable nonetheless before our journey to Polokwane, in a remote corner of South Africa. A win over Mexico might have papered over everything that wasn't working and transformed the atmosphere. But our 2-0 defeat exposed the cracks and left us teetering on the brink of being knocked out. At half-time, with the score 0–0, the void was not yet yawning beneath our feet, but we were already on a tightrope. We had been extremely skittish. As regards the incident in the half-time dressing room that sparked off the whole crisis, there was nothing new about it: Raymond Domenech had long rebuked Nicolas Anelka for dropping back very deep from his centre-forward position to seek the ball, leaving a hole at the front end. Nico, who played on the right for his club – and sometimes for Les Bleus too – had never been one to stay in position; he always liked to peel away. But when he dropped back to seek the ball, Franck Ribéry was already in that zone, so we were then undermanned to press forward and couldn't achieve anything decent. That's the background to the infamous half-time clash. In my view, it's pretty simple what happened: the manager told Nico off for peeling away, and Nico told him where to go, saying something like, 'Switch me if you're not happy.' To which the manager replied, 'Nico, you come off; Dédé [André-Pierre Gignac], you come on.' It was Nico's reaction, I think, that convinced Domenech to take him off. But there was nothing out of the ordinary about this reaction. Nico was disappointed and muttering to himself. In anger and frustration he slammed his boots down on the floor, and even though it wasn't a large dressing room, and we weren't that distant from each other, I didn't hear what he said. But Nico must have let slip something like, 'Do what you like with your shitty team.' Although, as I say, I don't know exactly because, like many of us there, I didn't hear it properly. I've been asked about it many times since, but I'm not a reliable enough witness. My impression was that he said it without defiance, in a calm, low voice in the quiet dressing room. When Raymond said, 'Go warm up, Dédé,' not for a single moment did I think that Nico had crossed a line. I've seen much worse scenes in my career, scenes which were followed by apologies the next day that would mark the end of the matter, and we'd carry on progressing as a team.

I don't know what impact this incident had on our second half, but Nico was a high-status player who had scored a decisive goal in our playoff in Dublin and had made a positive difference to our qualifying. From my place in goal, I'd had a perfect view of how the first half played out: apart from our issues at the front end, we'd showed a nervousness in defence, a feeling of being smothered by the Mexicans. We were always late to the ball, we never won a one-on-one, we were incapable of dictating the play, and we made a lot of mistakes. All of us were lacking, not just the forwards. Walking back onto the pitch for the second half, our good intentions would prove insufficient. We conceded a goal after bungling an offside trap, then a second. We now needed a miracle, a victory over South Africa with a two-goal difference while hoping that Uruguay would be defeated by Mexico, who had already gone through.

We were on the edge of the precipice and I was beside myself. In the mixed zone I could only manage a laconic, 'I prefer not to talk about it, otherwise I'll lose control.' I wasn't captain yet, I wasn't obliged to speak for the rest of the team, and I didn't want to badmouth them. At any rate, after the match, the incident between the head coach and Nico wasn't discussed around me. But for the entourage of Nico, Franck Ribéry, Thierry Henry and Éric Abidal, yes, it must have been.

We returned to Knysna very, very late at night. Friday found us in post-defeat doom and gloom. But it was Saturday when everything got tense, after the publication of that day's *L'Équipe* and Nico's expulsion from the squad. If the incident on Thursday night had been the real reason, he would have been expelled straight away. It wasn't. The front page of *L'Équipe*, with its extraordinarily crude headline ('Go Fuck Yourself, You Filthy Motherfucker') didn't match what I'd heard, but it did trigger Nico's sending home. From then on, Saturday went up in smoke. Pat Evra dashed about in vain to find Raymond to tell him that the squad stood firm with Nico, and that we didn't accept his expulsion. But he was never able to talk to him, the manager was lying low. The FFF (Fédération Française de Football) should have got a handle on things, defused the crisis situation, managed the media better and refocused the debate and our energy on our narrow chances of qualification. But no one from the Federation was there – or, rather, no one was capable of doing this, which amounted to precisely the same thing.

Isolated in that luxury hotel, and left to our own devices in the absence of people like Noël Le Graët (who would become FFF president a year later) or someone like Jean-Michel Aulas, who would have prevented us from losing our footing, we held meeting after meeting. In the first, Pat Evra explained the situation to us, and the squad was with him, agreeing that Nico shouldn't have been expelled. There was also the issue of apologies – Nico believed that he couldn't publicly apologize for something he hadn't said. As the hours passed, the leaders were emotionally overwhelmed by the injustice done to Nico. But these feelings distracted us from what should have been the prime concern: that, only 48 hours later, we had a World Cup match to play with an infinitesimal chance of qualifying – but a chance nonetheless. Nobody, inside or outside the team, was able to refocus us on the preparation for this game.

In the course of one of the meetings, on Saturday night,

there arose the question of what action we might take to show our support for Nico. The messy, lively debate concluded with the drafting of a press release and a decision not to go on a training strike, but simply to not train in front of the cameras and to remain indoors. It was a light training session, the kind we do two days before (and after) a match. Our collective anger had three targets: the Federation, which had taken the decision to expel Anelka from the squad under pressure; the media; and the manager, in whom we had lost all faith. We also mistrusted, by extension, the staff. Virtually eliminated, we began to realize that it would suit everyone to make us appear a bunch of yobs who, alone, were guilty, as if everybody wanted to already distance themselves in advance from the failure.

There was an initial version of the press release. Jérémy Toulalan suggested we get it rewritten, which was necessary. I wasn't heavily involved in all that, I had just arrived, but I could clearly see that the competition itself, which wasn't over, had taken second place to everything swirling around it. Our delegation wasn't the sort of strongly bonded squad I would be fortunate enough to know later. The explosion had come from an accumulation of things, big and small, and the split with Raymond only revealed deeper historic issues with certain players. In 2010 we carried the weight of a heritage. When I was first capped, I never had the feeling that I was joining a squad operating in a healthy atmosphere but, rather, one where everyone thought of themselves, and let the devil take the hindmost. It was never going to end well. Euro 2008 had gone badly, nothing was smooth and calm, and there wasn't enough leadership to protect the team from outside attacks. I still think that if Thierry Henry and Pat Vieira had played, and if Noël Le Graët or Jean-Michel Aulas had been with us, we would never have reached such a catastrophic point.

Since then, many have told me about the rumours surrounding the attitude of certain players to Yoann Gourcuff, but I saw nothing of the sort. I think mainly that Yo is a very reserved chap who doesn't open up to others easily, and didn't really have an off-pitch relationship with the bedrock of the team: Pat Evra, Franck Ribéry, Nicolas Anelka and Éric Abidal. He was an up-and-coming talent who'd pulled off some incredible feats at Bordeaux – champions of France the previous year – and the massive spotlight thrown on him wasn't much to the liking of players who'd had more responsibility in the French team for a while. But I noticed no ostracism on the pitch; it might have been his impression, but from where I was standing, I didn't see it.

And there were some invented stories too, such as the fight on the plane between Franck Ribéry and Yoann. Yet as false as that story was, it remains the reason for Franck

Ribéry's appearance on the *Téléfoot* TV show at the hotel that notorious Sunday. We were having a players' meeting at the same time and wondered, 'Where's Franck got to?' Having agreed we wouldn't speak to anyone, he hadn't been able to contain himself. Coming back from the show, he justified himself by explaining that all kinds of rubbish was being talked about him, and that it was affecting him deeply, his family too. He hadn't said anything about our deliberations, which would in fact continue to evolve.

We told ourselves: 'Hey, guys, there are fans who've come a long way. We can't not go down there.' We wanted to stay inside and demonstrate our discontent with the media, the FFF and the manager, but we couldn't do that to the fans. So we decided to head out to the practice pitch, sign some autographs and maybe have our press release read out. If it hadn't been for the fans, we'd have stayed inside and there wouldn't have been any strike in front of the world's live TV cameras.

I ran into the head coach in the hotel corridor on Sunday afternoon – after *Téléfoot* and our meeting – on my way back to my room. I think he was looking for information. I didn't tell him of our upcoming action, I just said, 'I'm sorry, coach, I can't break my solidarity with the squad, but I think we're going to do a foolish thing.' We were all pretty tense as we got off the bus at the practice pitch in

KNYSNA

mid-afternoon. We wanted to quickly sign autographs and get back on board. But when Pat Evra told fitness coach Robert Duverne that we wouldn't be training, the footage of their argument was all anyone could talk about – Robert went ballistic and had to be held back by Raymond, all on live TV. People wondered what was going on. So we got back on the bus, and it was all a disaster after that. I was sitting towards the front of the bus, a few seats behind the staff, to my left. The situation had become untenable. The staff didn't give the driver permission to move off because they thought they could reason with us and convince us to train. But then there was the press release, which the players didn't want to read themselves, and which would eventually be read out by a war weary Raymond Domenech. Nothing was going as we'd planned; we were completely losing control. Our plan had been simple, but it all became very complicated, and that was before we'd even realized what image it gave of the French national team to be seen going on strike in the middle of a World Cup. For us, it was simply a refusal to train in front of the media. For the rest of the world, it became quite another thing.

The scene in the bus was never-ending. The whole team demanded that we be taken back to the hotel, some players banged on the windows, and several people got on board to try to get us to change our minds. We did wonder, it's true, if it wouldn't be better to get off and run a bit, but we were cornered by the position we'd taken, with no other choice but to stay the course. I know all of the questions people ask today, about the players who could have stepped in to stop it. Would all this have happened if Thierry Henry had still been captain of the French team? I don't think so. But Titi was not cut out to be a substitute, he doesn't have the personality for it. When you pick him, it's to make him play, not to stick him on the bench. He may have had some difficulties for six months at Barça, but he was still capable of giving us a lot. The fact we were playing in this World Cup was also thanks to him, and not just because of his left hand. He was one of the four or five greatest French players in history. Can you imagine anyone daring to put Raymond Kopa, Michel Platini or Zinedine Zidane through something like that? You can't see them sitting quietly at the back of the bus in a squad led by other players.

There's so much else one could say. Tracing things back, and with the hindsight of all these years, I have a better understanding of how and why the Knysna affair played out as it did. But I still have the feeling that, setting aside our (huge) error, we were sacrificed. We were completely abandoned by the manager and the Federation, and we were attacked by the journalists. We had really solid arguments to explain the failure, but after the strike and that notorious

Sunday, they were swept aside by those powerful images and we were described as unmanageable, torpedoed by the journalists equally responsible for the crisis. Even today, I sometimes discuss it with some of them and we still don't agree. If it hadn't been for that headline, Nico would have finished the World Cup, which would have been a resounding sporting failure, but only a sporting one.

I know that the general public imagine that there were some white knights in the group, players opposed to the collective decision and who we forced to stay silent. But no, that wasn't the case. I didn't agree with Nico's eviction, and it wasn't the moment to break solidarity. Did we make the right choice? No. It was an error. We weren't thinking clearly about how our actions would be interpreted because we lived in a bubble, and this error swept us away. In fact, as far as we were concerned, it wasn't even the coach who had requested Nico's eviction, but the Federation. There was also that scene during the Saturday press conference with the Federation president, Jean-Pierre Escalettes, and Pat Evra, at a point where everyone was looking for the mole. I recall the words: 'There's a traitor among us.' With the benefit of experience, I know now that it's ridiculous to look for a mole. When you talk to your entourage or your agent, you can never know what they'll do with what you tell them.

EARNING MY SPURS

On the Monday, in Bloemfontein, the day after the strike and the day before the third match (against South Africa), Roselyne Bachelot, French Minister of Health and Sports, came to see us, intent on bringing some order, but she soon realized that she was dealing with calm, reasonable players who'd set out their arguments. She would later say that she made us cry, and call us 'immature yobbos' in the French parliament. She must have had quite some memory of our meeting, because I rather had the impression that it was a cordial exchange. I still wonder how she could have arrived at that conclusion.

The manager called us together in late afternoon: 'I'll be making choices, but if there are players who don't feel in a state to play, let them say so.' He had already spoken with Éric Abidal, who preferred not to play a last World Cup match. I don't judge him, because each one of us had our way of dealing with the awful collective situation. But we needed everybody to keep hope alive – at least until that faded during our 2-1 defeat to South Africa. We were drained by the tension, the stress and the pressure of all these events and couldn't withstand the hunger of the host country. Yoann Gourcuff got a red card in the first 30 minutes and I came out of goal a touch too soon at a corner to concede our first goal – not helped by those awful balls which were much too light because of the altitude. I made some decent saves after that, but there was nothing worth remembering about this match, which turned out to be Thierry Henry's last with the French national team.

Scars and injuries are what remain of the 2010 World Cup. Nothing was the same between the players and the press afterwards, and social media didn't help. I was fortunate, at least, to experience what this failure unleashed: Noël Le Graët took over at the FFF and rebuilt everything. The trio he formed with Didier Deschamps and Florence Hardouin was key to this reconstruction, even if it ended badly.

Later on, when I became captain, I remembered Knysna and the importance of the relationship between a manager and a team's stalwarts. I've always tried to be a very balanced captain. I have never got too ecstatic in moments of joy, or too low in moments of crisis, which has allowed me to stay on track. In Knysna the circumstances made Pat Evra a highly emotional and somewhat blinkered captain, determined to go all the way once he'd made his mind up. Everything that had been an attribute in his career, everything which allowed him to get that far, turned into a flaw for those few days. His leadership was very intense in all his teams. That's not a criticism – it was a positive thing most of the time – but perhaps we didn't need so much intensity at a point where we had totally lost perspective, blinded by our internal issues, not keeping in mind everything else that was happening. Sunday evening, after the strike, as phones rang in the players' rooms and the shocking realization of what had just happened began to dawn, my father was constructive and clear-headed amid the storm: 'You really must have been abandoned to end up in such a place. You found yourselves all alone.' All alone indeed, but together for once, that summer.

X

A Cup

We had to get over Knysna. The media were waiting for us at the airport when myself and the other OL players returned to Lyon from South Africa, and a guy pretended to throw an egg in our direction, which we didn't find very funny. I don't recall our goodbyes to the manager in Paris, but it can't have been very friendly. I was 23, keen to turn the page, and I told myself that maybe I would get another opportunity to play in a World Cup. Marine was pregnant and I went away to Corsica for a week with my father, my brother and some friends. I was afraid of how people might look at me, and I was apprehensive about seeing my friends and family, but in Corsica nobody bothered me regarding the World Cup.

The media and the political class demanded we be sanctioned. It was an awful summer for Jérémy Toulalan, and he didn't deserve it. Anelka had been given an 18-match ban by the Federation, and Ribery a three-match ban, for their parts in the Knysna affair, but Toulalan received a one-match ban for having asked his agent to redraft the squad's press release. His intervention came from a good place: he only wanted people to stop chatting rubbish about the team and for us to at least control our own communication. Toul is a diamond, and he really suffered from this whole business. He was 26 in South Africa and never played for France again. But he was a wonderful player and went on to play some beautiful football, particularly at Málaga and Monaco. We were all suspended for at least one match, and we all lost our bonuses, which was to be expected, given the flight of several sponsors and the impact on the image of the French national team.

The return to league football at Lyon should have helped us forget Knysna. But Toul, unjustly sent before a disciplinary commission, and Yoann Gourcuff, who had just arrived at OL, were both deeply affected. Yoann's public presentation at Gerland was the last thing he needed. Yo has always found it hard to bear this burden, and he has a particular relationship with fame, and even with competition. We had a chat before his signing, which I had encouraged him to do, but his five years at Lyon were bumpy. I think he was a victim of his own success. He had everything going for him, did some incredible things on the pitch and was promised an exceptional future, but he had to deal with everything at the same time: the fallout from Knysna, the expectations, his transfer fee. His body held him back and he entered a vicious circle that never enabled him to get back on top, physically or mentally. When he was in a good place, he pulled off some superb performances, but after two years of walking on water at Bordeaux, the bar was set very high. Yo is a lovely chap, but top-flight competition shows no mercy to self-doubt or the slightest form of weakness. The situation created difficulties not only for the club's finances but also in the dressing room, where everyone else went out to fight for points while Yo sought to get his feel for the ball back.

I forged a protective shell around myself as regards Knysna, and carried on. And it no doubt made it easier for me because I was unscathed. It was a long, hard season for Olympique Lyonnais. Late September found us losing the 100th derby against Saint-Étienne (0-1) after an unbelievable free-kick from Dimitri Payet, before slipping down to 14th place in the league and heading for crisis territory. But this defeat didn't affect me the same way it would have done a few days earlier or later: three days before the derby, our daughter Anna-Rose was born in Tassin-la-Demi-Lune, north of Lyon, not far from our house in Limonest. It was a huge event for us and brought us tremendous joy, which really helped me put things in perspective.

A CUP

As the defeats piled up, the fans began to turn against the manager, Claude Puel. A weight, a negative energy, oppressed us all season long. But we hung on in there, pulled ourselves back up the table and swiped third place after the final match in Monaco, thanks to a win which would relegate AS Monaco – Claude Puel's cherished home team – but save Nice, to my great joy.

Even though this recovery was ours, first and foremost, I always admired how Jean-Michel Aulas managed the crisis. Nothing was going right: he had made huge financial investments and was still waiting for his project to build a new, larger stadium to get off the ground; he was stymied by Claude's long-term contract; and the fans were starting to grumble. But it was within the club's genes and the chairman's abilities to handle crises and save a season like that. Aulas attended every match and every pre-match meeting, which was a means of exerting pressure on the players and the manager while making it clear that he wouldn't give up. He constantly reminded us what the Champions League represented for the club, and, despite the conflicts and tensions with the fans, he made us realize that we had to stick to our guiding principles. And that we had to make these efforts for us and for our future. In times of crisis, the level of commitment and expectation is higher with Jean-Michel than at any other club, and that's how we finished a season we'd messed up in third place. But Jean-Michel was also a chairman who had considerable respect for his players, who always listened to them – even though that didn't stop him summoning them for a dressing down. He also held meetings to try to understand why it wasn't working with Yoann, and how we could help him. He was always a constructive chairman; he was the face of the club, the one carrying everything on his shoulders. At the Olympique Lyonnais of those days you never felt you were alone. I have enormous respect and admiration for Jean-Michel Aulas, and I have always had a good relationship with him. If OL hadn't needed the cash from my transfer, in summer 2012, I might well have stayed another year. I love the way he defended the interests of his club, the way he took blows for others. His leadership protected everyone.

Whenever Jean-Michel Aulas was with us, his right-hand man, Bernard Lacombe, was never far away. He was rather more feared in the dressing room, particularly for his quips in the press or on the club's TV channel, but I had an excellent relationship with Bernard from the very first day. He liked to be there for the players, mainly because it was the game which interested him, and he always had stories to tell. He was very kind to those who gave their all for the club, but if you cheated, you'd find yourself the target of his withering wit. The other players had told me about his comments on OL TV before I arrived – they were rather raw, no filter. But he was rarely wrong because he knew his football – he had played close to 500 games as a striker for Lyon and Bordeaux in the 1970s and 1980s. If he said of a player that they had played a decent match, it wasn't a compliment.

At Lyon I extended my contract on my own, without an agent. I'd had one briefly in 2007, to manage the end of my season at Nice, to save me and my father the fuss. But when I arrived at OL in 2008, and they gave me their proposed figures, I didn't negotiate: I was multiplying by four a contract that I had already extended at Nice with good conditions. I told myself that if I was good, I would be paid accordingly. I'm not sure that I would have had better contracts if I had had an agent. Perhaps they would have opened other doors for me, but I preferred to open them myself, and that was really easy to do at Lyon. To extend my contract in 2011 I went to see the chairman at his IT firm, Cegid, beside the River Saône, and we didn't even talk numbers. It was Vincent Ponsot, his general director, who did so by phone. We didn't spend all night on it either. Vincent Ponsot called me one evening, as I was relaxing on my terrace in Limonest, to ask me for 'my figures', as he put it. Having become the incumbent keeper of the French national team, my status at the club had also changed so I proposed we double my salary. All he replied was: 'I'll speak to the boss and get back to you.' The answer was very soon in coming, and it was a 'yes'. I knew what the others were earning. There was Licha, and Yoann a little above him with his Adidas contract, but I was in the top three salaries and I didn't need an agent to push for ten per cent more, which he would have taken as commission. One year later, when I left for Tottenham, the English club appointed a French agent, but I made it simple and requested the same contract as at OL – not a pound more or a pound less.

Claude Puel was fired in 2011, following our third-place finish. He didn't do everything right, but you could never accuse him of throwing in the towel. He gave everything, never lost his commitment and went through some really tough, even painful periods in a brutal atmosphere. He didn't win a trophy, but he succeeded in maintaining OL in the Champions League for three consecutive seasons. I ran into him in the Premier League later, and I hold him in high esteem. In football, we're all just passing through – it works, or it doesn't work – but I have nothing bad to say about Claude: he believed in me, he gave me my first armbands for cup matches, and he helped mould me into the player I became. It was Claude who made me realize how hard the job of manager really is. Previously, I was focused on myself and I didn't yet have an overview of how you manage a staff, a squad, different cultures and egos, clans and problematic coexistences – issues that can result in an overly rigid methodology. But the players never gave up on him either. We respected his endurance despite the jibes, the personal graffiti on the city's walls, the hostility in the stadium. None of which helped the team, but we held firm. Three years he stayed, and even though he took us to second in the league, and third twice, the lack of silverware grated on the fans.

Rémi Garde was appointed manager in June 2011 and I really liked that season with him. He'd been scouting director when I'd arrived at the club, and we clicked. Former midfielder and upcoming manager Bruno Génésio was there, fitness coach Robert Duverne was returning, Joël Bats continued in post and former striker Gérald Baticle joined us, having been promoted from managing the under-19s. I told myself that I felt like staying at OL with these people I got on well with. In the Champions League we again found ourselves in the same group as Real Madrid, who would beat us twice (4–0 and 0–2). It was the Real of José Mourinho, who'd already knocked us out the previous season in the round of 16 (1–1 then 3–0). Indeed, Mourinho had approached me to ask: 'Can I have your shirt at the end of the match? My son loves goalies and he likes you a lot.' Obviously I wondered if it was sincere or fake, in light of the character and the legend around him. But I gladly gave it to him. He thanked me and promised to give me one in return. At the end of the second leg, someone came to tell me, 'José Mourinho's waiting outside the dressing room for you.' There he was, holding a Real shirt on which he had written a few words expressing his admiration and wishing me the best. I could never imagine that he would become my manager one day.

Yet again, we qualified for the Champions League round of 16, this time after a miracle victory in Zagreb (1–7) during the final group game, but we were immensely disappointed to be knocked out by APOEL Nicosia on penalties (after two 1–0 results). We should have been among the eight best European teams that season. To nab a trophy, I was counting on the final of the League Cup, in April, against Olympique de Marseille, but we conceded a goal from Brandão in extra time (1–0) at the Stade de France. At least we were able to return to the same venue two weeks later for the final of the Coupe de France, where we beat Quevilly 1–0, thanks to a goal from Lisandro, and I finally won the first trophy of my professional career. That we had won the Coupe de France against a team from the third division, two levels below us in Ligue 1, took the edge off neither our joy nor

A CUP

our pride, because we'd eliminated Bordeaux 3–1 in extra time in the round of 16, not to mention pulling off the feat of beating PSG 1–3 in the quarter-finals at Parc des Princes. If we weren't playing a big fish in the final, that's because we had beaten them all already. I finally got to experience the fervour of a reception on the balcony of Lyon town hall overlooking Place des Terreaux, where Olympique Lyonnais had celebrated all of their French championship titles. A Coupe de France wasn't what I'd been hoping for when I arrived in Lyon, but 12 years later it remains the club's last trophy, with the exception of that year's Trophée des Champions, which was played in New Jersey and where we beat Montpellier 4–2 on penalties (after drawing 2–2), just before I left Lyon.

As poignant as it was to leave OL and our Limonest bolthole, I was excited to be heading for London and Tottenham Hotspur. A new club and a new world.

XI

Captain

I wore the armband of the captain of the French national team for the first time on 17 November 2010 at Wembley, where we beat England 1–2, with my father watching from the stands. The armband didn't have slogans printed on it back then: it was blue, white and red. Simple. Magnificent. Laurent Blanc, who had replaced Raymond Domenech, had passed the captaincy between several team stalwarts in the first few months of his term as manager. I was 23, which was young to be captain, but I never even wondered whether it would change anything in how I played or my life as an international. I remained obsessed with my own performance – that was my priority. From 2010 to Euro 2012 I never felt like a captain, just a leader in a team finding itself in order to rebuild – but these years would encompass the second most wonderful period of invincibility in the history of the French national team. Out of the ruins of

CAPTAIN

Knysna this team played 27 matches in succession without defeat, from losing at home to Belarus (0–1) in September 2010 to defeat in Sweden (2–0) in June 2012.

I was the leader, but I wasn't very vocal yet. That's never seemed contradictory to me. I don't know if one is born a leader, but I imagine that there are signs. I wasn't very outgoing earlier on in my career, but I listened a lot. At Nice, Fred Antonetti liked to ask how we felt about the previous day's match. Aged 19, I had to pipe up in front of everyone. Just like with the press, I was always more relaxed post-match. Pre-match, I don't have much to say, unless there is something very specific to get across. But there are exceptions, such as at Tottenham during Antonio Conte's first season, just before playing at home to Arsenal, who we thrashed 3–0: 'Imagine for just one moment if Arsenal came and beat us here, at home, swiping our fourth place and qualifying for the Champions League, in front of our fans. It's impossible, it can't happen!' But when you play 50 matches in the season, you don't always have something to say.

At Lyon, Claude Puel, too, liked asking players to express themselves, particularly when things were going less well. That's maybe why he gave me the armband for several matches. When Rémi Garde took over the team in 2011 he dithered, knowing that I was sometimes captain of the

French national team, but then he told me, 'Listen, I don't want you to take it badly. It's not at all something against you, because I know I can count on you and that you could be captain. But I would prefer [the captain] to be an outfield player, namely Licha, because of what he represents.' I put my hand on his shoulder and reassured him: 'No problem as far as I'm concerned, it doesn't change a thing. I don't need to wear the armband. I'm with you, ready to help, to give my all.' Looking back on it, I realize that, as a youngster, people discerned a sense of duty in me, a sense of responsibility, certainly leadership. But over the first part of my career I was so focused on my objectives that I never sought the captaincy. Things came naturally.

No doubt you need to wait until you're 24 or 25 to start to know yourself well. Captaincy is something to be learned, it doesn't come straight away. You have to know what it entails and take on board the symbolic value and the real responsibility, which at national level are greater than what you might feel at a club.

Laurent Blanc made his decision in February 2012, before an away match against Germany (which we won 1-2). I remain convinced that Eric Abidal would have been his captain, were it not for his illness and the liver transplant which kept him out of play for more than a year. Rotating it between us had worked well up until then. Alou Diarra was

CAPTAIN

captain eight times; and Philippe Mexès, Flo Malouda and Samir Nasri were captains too; but it was me the manager chose. I was 25, Germany–France was my 31st cap and I was captain for the seventh time. Laurent Blanc came to Lyon to give me the news, but without really saying so. I met him at Lyon-Saint Exupéry Airport, where he informed me that I was one of three potential captains, but that he hadn't made up his mind. When he did, I became captain of the French national team for good. I told myself I wouldn't let it change me, but the truth is that I didn't necessarily feel ready for it. I felt that I hadn't lived enough yet to guide a team. Indeed, Didier Deschamps became captain of Les Bleus at 28, and Zinedine Zidane at 32. That's no accident. But then I thought that my personality must have come into it and that they surely chose me for a reason.

My relationship with Laurent Blanc didn't change with the armband. I wasn't yet the representative of the other players, and everything was still quite turbulent around us: the manager and the FFF had been shaken by the storm which blew up around quotas (it had been proposed that no more than 50 per cent of youngsters taken on at the Clairefontaine national training centre should hold double nationality). We were slowly recovering from Knysna and I tried not to go off-topic in front of the press: just talk about the pitch, protect the team, protect my teammates.

I went to press conferences with the coach, but we didn't indulge in big discussions. Not because of him, only that, at my age, I lacked the self-confidence to talk about anything and everything with the manager, as I would do later with Didier Deschamps. Laurent Blanc only stayed two years, which went quickly, but I would have liked to have got to know him better because he's someone who left his mark on the history of French football. His assistant, Jean-Louis Gasset, was closer to us, owing to his role and his temperament. Everyone adored him. He brought a liveliness to training sessions, was approachable and had an unbelievable naturalness, with his accent from down Montpellier way, and he loved his players. His speech-making was amazing too: when he spoke on the morning of a match, you felt like playing straight away.

Euro 2012 was much more positive than the World Cup 2010 – which wasn't hard – but it was not as successful as we had hoped. Losing the quarter-final 2–0 to Spain – the European and World champions – was surely nothing to be ashamed of, but we spent three weeks in Ukraine without totally ridding ourselves of the millstone of Knysna. The polemic was present in the first match against England (1–1), when Samir equalized and celebrated the goal in his own way, by putting a finger to his lips while staring down the press box. Then, in the mixed zone, he got involved in an incident with a journalist. He spoke rudely to the guy, but the journalist had provoked him by saying, 'Get lost.' The perfect answer to something like that is always to be found on the pitch; and that was my takeaway as captain.

Apart from the massive storm which delayed kick-off before our beautiful 2–0 victory over Andriy Shevchenko's Ukraine, we had the indecencyto lose our focus, and the match, against Zlatan Ibrahimović's Sweden (2–0), with a modified team, when we were already all but qualified. This defeat provoked tensions in the dressing room. The squad comprised huge talents, but there were some big egos – too many, no doubt. It's the eternal question: should one build a squad by taking the best players? Or should one build a squad to have the best team? It's an issue for all managers, who don't all settle it the same way. In Ukraine the defeat to Sweden aroused frustrations in those who weren't playing. In and of itself, the defeat wasn't so serious – even though it sent us into that quarter-final against Spain – but after 20 months without losing, you should never disregard a defeat because they all happen for a reason; every detail counts and a team can malfunction at any moment. Which is what happened with us. We felt it, as the quarter-final drew closer, and things got complicated because Laurent Blanc made bold choices, switching to a 3-5-2 formation. Players such as Samir were victims of this change, and there were too many egos, yet again, to stand firm as a squad against our opponent. Our 2-0 defeat, and everything that went with it, was unfortunately seen in the light of what had occurred in South Africa, as if everyone was waiting to blow on the embers which we believed were extinguished.

Three incidents in particular set tongues a-wagging, one of which involved me. The first arose when Hatem Ben Arfa, who had barely returned to the dressing room after the defeat, answered his ringing phone and began chatting away, provoking a heated conversation between him and the coach, whom Hatem resented for his selection decisions and blamed for having substituted him in the sole match where he'd made the starting line-up. It hardly lightened the mood, but that evening they shook hands and we all moved on, forgetting that once these things get out in the press they become uncontrollable. In days gone by, what happened in the dressing room stayed in the dressing room. That hasn't been the case for some time now – and is how the dustup between Samir Nasri and Alou Diarra during Euro 2012 blew up out of all proportion: yes, they argued, but they greeted each other the next day like normal. You can fly off the handle, you can even come to blows – I've seen it – but that wasn't the case in Donetsk. The problem is that such scenes are misinterpreted from the outside and, if given prolonged focus, as in this case, maintain tensions that the players would otherwise very shortly forget. In Ukraine, this obviously rubbed off on such a young and fragile squad.

The final incident – zoomed in on by the TV cameras – involved Jérémy Ménez insulting me on the pitch. He came across as a brat and was even suspended when, to be frank, it was me who started it and had given him a bollocking. I had been correct to do so: on the pitch, you don't have time to say, 'Please,' or 'Pardon me,' or discuss things over a genteel cuppa, so you snipe at each other – but at the end it's forgotten. I didn't want to play the decent chap in this affair; I thought that we really needed to be done with Mr Nice Guy, Mr Polite Guy, the cherub-faced kid. So I defended Jérémy publicly, and it did no good at all, sadly. He was suspended, which was quite ridiculous. I didn't like this two-year chapter of the French team being boiled down to these incidents. We deserved better than such conflations, having played 27 matches without losing. We didn't deserve it when the slightest defeat was used to dredge up the demons and portrayals of the past. We didn't deserve being considered good guys only when we were winning.

XII

Hugo Who?

I hesitated between Arsenal and Tottenham. Arsène Wenger had pushed hard initially, calling me twice in ten days before opting for an internal choice. He let me know with considerable class. I saw him regularly at France matches because he was a consultant for TF1, but we had never spoken about a move. Marine and I got married in the summer of 2012, before honeymooning in Venice. But having hoped that the transfer would go through fast, it seemed to take an age. Daniel Levy, the Tottenham boss, whom I would get to know well, always tries to push transfer prices as far down as he can, waiting for the last moments of the transfer window to ramp up the pressure and make the other party believe that he won't buy. I experienced something of a rollercoaster before being transferred for 10 million euros plus bonuses – a 15 million euro deal in total. Mid-August, when I'd already agreed terms with Spurs, Jean-Michel

HUGO WHO?

Aulas and Vincent Ponsot told me that Tottenham had still not contacted Olympique Lyonnais, meaning that I actually commenced the next season with Lyon. After the second day, Tottenham and OL finally reached an agreement, but the English club left us with no news for two days while I was in the middle of trying to sort out the logistics of my move. On the third day, Tottenham got back in touch with a lower offer and Jean-Michel Aulas cancelled the whole shebang, calling me to say that he was sorry and that OL were not responsible for the situation, which I, of course, understood. Twenty-four hours later Tottenham accepted Lyon's terms, and this time Jean-Michel Aulas left the choice up to me, given how things had gone. But my thoughts hadn't changed: this was the moment to try something different. I flew out to London in a mad rush on 31 August to sign my contract. I had my medical check-up at Tottenham's old training centre, where I met Daniel Levy as well as André Villas-Boas, the manager, and his staff. They wanted to present me to the fans on the Saturday against Norwich, but I told them that I needed to say goodbye to the OL fans at the match against Valenciennes that same day – I didn't want to leave Lyon like a thief in the night – which they understood.

Tottenham chartered a private jet to bring me over after trying to negotiate with OL to split the costs, but they made me fly back to Lyon on EasyJet. Which didn't bother me, it just made me smile.

It was hard to leave Lyon. I'd put my feelings to one side while I made up my mind, but upon returning to Gerland to say goodbye, I was filled with emotion. I realized that I would miss them all terribly: Joël Bats, the chairman, Licha, the players, the staff and the fans, who had always supported me. I can see myself now, a little before kick-off, holding Anna-Rose, with Licha and Jean-Michel Aulas right beside me. We didn't speak, we were just very moved. After the match, I did the lap of honour with Anna-Rose in my arms, then I went home to watch my new club Tottenham draw 1–1 with Norwich, and I heard my new manager André Villas-Boas say, 'Brad Friedel is the number 1 goalkeeper.' Which was a good start . . .

I very quickly came to realize that this transfer suited no one. Brad Friedel had just finished a great season and Villas-Boas didn't necessarily wish to take any risks with regard to a pillar of the dressing room. It made no difference that I was captain of the French national team, or that I had played 30 matches in the Champions League, I still had to wait. I didn't like waiting and I didn't like being told that I had time. I'm a rational fellow: whenever I have a choice to make, I imagine the worst-case scenario so as not to be surprised. But this scenario, I didn't see coming.

HUGO WHO?

I was number 2 and I spent two months in a hotel, alone, the time it took to find a house so that Marine and Anna-Rose could join me. Above all, I realized that I was the chairman's pick not the manager's – whom I had tried to talk to during the negotiations, but in vain.

André Villas-Boas was coming off the back of a season at Chelsea where he had been sacked after losing the dressing room while trying to assert his authority with regard to several longstanding players. Arriving at Tottenham, he had therefore decided to keep Brad Friedel, a good goalie whom I respect enormously. It really wasn't him that was the problem, but the club, who hadn't been transparent. I'd wanted a challenge and, my goodness, did I get one! I felt truly alone, and I asked myself: 'Why on earth did I board that plane?' I would train all week only to sit on the bench all weekend; it rained non-stop, you never saw the sky, and I was stuck in a hotel an hour and a quarter from the city centre.

Having departed Lyon to the roar of 40,000 fans at Gerland, I had become anonymous again at a team where the manager didn't want me. The situation was very slow to evolve. Although I was picked quite quickly to play against Lazio in the Europa League (a clean sheet, we drew 0-0), assailed by my doubts and my solitude I was then benched again, and after a good debut in the Premier League against Aston Villa (2–0) on 7 October, my hopes that things were moving forward were dashed before the following match when, looking at the flipchart during the coach's talk, I read: 'Substitute: Lloris.' I really had the sensation, that autumn, that I was starting from zero. Luckily, the Frenchies in the squad, William Gallas and Younès Kaboul, gave me some support. William was different: I found him relaxed, gracious, and he helped me to adapt and wait for my hour to come. The French players at Arsenal – Laurent Koscielny, Olivier Giroud, Sébastien Squillaci and Bacary Sagna – were never far away either. On 23 September, Anna-Rose's birthday, Marine and Anna-Rose stayed with the Sagna family for three days, and we celebrated her second birthday there. My adaptation to London got a lot better once I found a house in Hadley Wood, a 15-minute drive from the training centre in Enfield. There, Marine and I created a new bolthole for ourselves and Anna-Rose, which helped to stabilize me and get over the short period when I didn't play. I never took the Tube as much as I did then – central London being only 20 minutes away on the Northern Line (the black one for those who know). And I could still go about incognito.

My hour came in late November, but even after having announced my place in the starting line-up, Villas-Boas continued to tell the press that he hadn't made his decision and that Brad Friedel could return at any moment. It was a tricky situation for everyone: for the manager, who hadn't wanted me, and for Friedel, who had seen his record-breaking streak of 310 consecutive appearances in the Premier League – a record he still holds – interrupted by me. I trained with Carlo Cudicini, Heurelho Gomes and Brad. It was top-flight stuff, and we respected each other (they are all upstanding chaps), but that period reminded me how much I couldn't stand being number 2. My temperament won't allow it; it's too far off what I want. Since I had played an official match for OL in August, I couldn't even request to be let go during the January transfer window because you're not allowed to play for three clubs in the same season. In England, you're nobody until you've proved that you are someone. There were plenty of obstacles for me to overcome.

My relations with Villas-Boas are good these days, but there was some friction a few times, particularly when he benched me even though I'd played against Aston Villa before the October international break. At the time, I was like any other player left out of the starting line-up: frustrated and angry. Truth be told, I felt like doing him over. But reason got the better of me: I wasn't going to cause a ruckus the day before a match. Still, I went to see him in his office first thing Monday, and said something along the lines of, 'When I signed here, I was promised something else. I have nothing against Brad, but you're wrecking my career. I have a certain status in France and I simply can't comprehend what you're trying to do. Why play me against Aston Villa and then, for the next match six days later, put me on the bench without warning me, without telling me anything?' There was nothing he could really say to that. In the weeks that followed, he often tried to speak to me, and I shunned him. When I returned to the club after the November international break, I ran into Tony Parks, the goalie coach, who told me, somewhat excitedly, 'Hugo, the manager wants to talk to you.' That day, Villas-Boas informed me I'd be starting against Arsenal, where we conceded five goals.

At that point, I could never have imagined that I'd spend the next 12 years at Tottenham. As calm as I tried to be about the situation, I often wondered: 'What have I done? Why did I leave a club where there was mutual appreciation and where I had responsibilities?' I asked myself this regularly, to be honest, over the next two years, until the arrival of Mauricio Pochettino.

Even though Olympique Lyonnais weren't quite as strong as they had been, they remained a great European club: well structured, led by a strong figure who controlled everything. At Tottenham we didn't know who was who or who controlled what, and the atmosphere was different: unlike in France, the English don't shake your hand when they walk in a room; everyone just gets on with their business. I even had the feeling that the manager was abandoned, left to his own devices, in front of the squad of players. I put in some good performances that first season, and I started to become known, but we imploded in full flight during the second season with the sacking of André Villas-Boas and the arrival of Tim Sherwood. I saw no future at the club.

By the summer of 2014, I'd had enough. I wanted to leave, so much so that Daniel Levy, who tried to convince me to stay, pulled me aside and told me confidentially, 'Mauricio Pochettino's arriving. You need to see him, have a chat with him. I want you to stay, you represent the new Tottenham. But if you stay, you extend your contract.' Mauricio and I clicked from the get-go. I found a direction again, a real philosophy of playing, a structure; a true way of working. I would also relish time spent with a new goalie coach, Toni Jiménez, with whom I became very close. He had been Olympic champion with Spain in 1992 and his opinion mattered much more to me than those who, oddly, judged me to be too short at 6 foot 2 inches (1.88m). One such critic was Christophe Lollichon, the Chelsea goalie coach, who saw only my flaws and compared me to Simon Pouplin when he trained him in Rennes. He went on and on about it all the time. He also said that I would never succeed in England. Strange, isn't it, that the man who appears most often in the French media talking about goalies should always find it hard to say anything positive about a keeper who's been capped 145 times for France? Time must pass very slowly for him.

One thing that I absolutely loved at Tottenham from the moment I arrived was their stadium, White Hart Lane. It was smaller than Gerland, but very compact, with a shorter pitch, and you felt that it had real soul. I adapted to the rough and tumble of the Premier League, where the referees only blow their whistle on obvious fouls. The penalty box became a new world for me. In France, I could have a bit of space to move about in, but in England, the merest sniff of a set piece would see a guy in front of me and one behind, whom the referee would let do what they liked. In France, on aerial balls, I would leave my goal to grab the ball because the ref would blow their whistle at the merest contact, but in England I quickly realized that I had to punch the balls away and only come out of the goal if I was absolutely sure. At Nice, and at Lyon, I was able to, not exactly roam about at will, but I could take risks. In England, this was no longer possible. And I was faced with the unbelievable quality of the centre-forwards, as well as a high number of players in the penalty area, which obliges you to process much more information at once. Everything was much faster, intense and unpredictable – but, let me be clear: it was fantastic!

I also discovered the practice of playing over the festive season. My birthday being 26 December I often celebrated it with a Boxing Day match – none of which I ever lost, as far as I can recall. I remember one game in 2015, during the Pochettino era, against Norwich (3–0), where, after several major saves, the whole stadium sang 'Happy Birthday' in the last ten minutes.

XIII

Brazil!

Summer 2012. Noël Le Graët, President of the French Football Federation phoned to let me know, in my capacity as captain (and before it became official), that Didier Deschamps would be taking over as manager of the French national team. Following in the footsteps of Laurent Blanc, who reinfused Les Bleus with a positive dynamic and could take credit for his role in their reconstruction, Didier was a major figure in French football. And he was a class act from the very first friendly match in August against Uruguay (0–0) at Le Havre, calling me into his room to chat for ten minutes, expressing his confidence in me and mentioning the captain's armband: 'It's fine with me for the moment, but things can always change. I need to see how the other players fare.' He wasn't casting doubt on my captaincy, he just wanted to forge his own team. And even though I'd had the armband for 15 matches by

BRAZIL!

then, I didn't take it badly; on the contrary, I appreciated his frankness and honesty. He wasn't saying that he was going to take it off me, only that his ideas might change. He finally appointed me as 'his' captain in January 2013, which didn't change anything as far as I was concerned. The captaincy was never an ambition for me, or an obsession, and I never thought I'd be captain for ten years. You'd have been mad to think I'd end up wearing the armband over 100 times. My primary goal was to attain a level with the national team that I had never reached before. I was at a very good level, but I wanted more, I wanted to be decisive in the final stages of competitions and to experience thrilling moments. At Euro 2012 my performances had been decent, but, in the context of the squad, rather flat; they'd gone unnoticed or had been quickly forgotten.

From 2008 to 2012, my first four years with Les Bleus, there had never been any stability. There was always something going on and we never felt very at ease when we arrived at Clairefontaine. We were still seeking a sense of fulfilment and a confidence, which would come later. It would take me 50 caps, I think, to feel I was part of a French national team that was actually popular. That all began one evening at the Stade de France in November 2013, during a World Cup playoff against Ukraine.

Didier Deschamps' arrival as manager coincided with my

departure for Tottenham. Not playing for the first three months at my new club somewhat took the edge off my game, but Didier kept his confidence in me and supported me, which was significant given the situation. To avoid the playoffs and qualify directly for the 2014 World Cup in Brazil, we would need to finish in front of Spain in our group, and we made a good show of it in Madrid in October 2012, playing in Atlético's old city-centre stadium, Vicente Calderón, its worn concrete imbuing it with a certain soul. Spain, double European champions and World Cup winners, were leading us 1–0, before half-time – and it would have been more had I not saved a penalty by Cesc Fàbregas. and had Olivier Giroud not equalized at the end of the match. It was a match full of hope, given that Spain had walked all over us in the Euros just four months earlier. It had been many a long year since Les Bleus had played such a robust match against an opponent of this calibre. Unfortunately we caved in the return match, sending us into the playoffs after the June 2013 tour of Uruguay and Brazil. I don't know if I would ever have visited Montevideo had the beautiful game not taken me there. It's always the same story when it comes to end-of-season tours: bodies and minds are tired and some people are obliged to play matches where they have more to lose than to gain. So the play wasn't that interesting, but they were lovely trips. From South America

BRAZIL!

I heard rumours of my transfer to Monaco, to which I replied that I was too much of a Niçois to contemplate such a move. These were indirect approaches, but I hadn't done all that I had – move to Lyon, then into the Premier League – to return to play 20 kilometres from home.

Montevideo aside, the blue strip enabled me to see lesser-known places where you don't go as a club player, or on holiday, as a rule, such as Tbilisi in Georgia or Homyel in Belarus, where statues of Lenin and Stalin still stand. I do have an awful memory of Homyel, though, owing to a terrible stomach bug, where the illusion of it getting better with the warm-up and adrenaline didn't last. I was dead – no energy – and everyone could see it: I messed up on two goals, luckily without consequence (we won 2–4), but I didn't like it at all.

Before the World Cup playoff against Ireland in 2009 I conceded five goals against Olympique de Marseille (5–5). Before the World Cup playoff against Ukraine in 2013 I received a bash on the head from Romelu Lukaku's knee one Saturday afternoon at Everton. In the 77th minute of that match, I came out of goal to meet a long ball and was ahead of him when his knee dragged, hitting me hard in the head. I blacked out for a few seconds. Coming round to the arrival of the medical staff, I was only aware of a sudden terrible pain in my head, not realizing that I had lost consciousness. I had the impression that I was answering their questions normally: 'What's the score?' 'What day is it?' In reality, I was hesitant, still stunned. The doctor tried to take me to the side of the pitch, as you could see clearly in the TV pictures, but I refused. You could read on my lips: 'I'm OK.' So I remained on the pitch and finished the match. I made one save and one clearance, and I thought everything was fine. It was when I got back to the dressing room and sat down that I really had a fright: a total blank. I couldn't remember anything at all. I started to panic, particularly because I was experiencing dizziness too. Back in London, I had a scan at hospital which reassured me. Everything was fine, except my memory. Rewatching the match helped me to retrieve it and to put my mind in order. I don't know if I actually recalled what happened, or if my brain was recording the images as if they were a new memory, but at least it helped me fill in the blanks. It was only afterwards that we followed the concussion protocol, and I didn't line up against Newcastle (just before the playoffs) because we'd done everything backwards: I should have come off at Everton to be able to play the following match. André Villas-Boas was criticized for having lauded my courage and heroism in playing on, given the new sensitivity to concussion that was developing in the UK. Since that day, I've always promised myself to leave the pitch of my own accord if it ever happens to me again – especially once the consequences of a concussion (in particular for rugby players) had been clearly explained to me. I would rewatch the images of the blow at Goodison Park at the beginning of every season when the club's doctors went over the concussion protocols with the squad, using this incident by way of illustration.

It wasn't the best way to prepare for the playoffs, 11 days before the first leg in Ukraine. In Kyiv we might have lost it all, the atmosphere was so crazy. We could feel the hostility, and hear it too. Nil-nil at half-time, I had the sense that we didn't realize the gravity of the situation, and I'm pretty sure I must have yelled a bit in the dressing room. A World Cup playoff is not a question of talent. After conceding the first goal, instead of remaining calm we completely opened ourselves up, creating spaces for the adversary, and at 2–0, when we were hanging by a thread and Laurent Koscielny had been sent off, we were still seeking to score an away goal. The truth is that we'd completely lost control, that it could have been worse, and that we were in a real fix.

The initial feeling in the dressing room after the match was one of catastrophe. In the debrief of this first leg, the manager gave us a lashing. But in the showers, we were already starting to discuss the return match. We'd been trampled on and we had three days to turn it all around.

The first thing to do was to start to believe that it was possible. What I particularly liked was that we took the defeat on the chin and immediately sought solutions. Fine, we'd lost – now what do we do? We knew not to wait for the match to come to us. All of our discussions and our detailed analysis of the game increased our hopes, little by little. I can see me now, with the Lyon midfielder Clément Grenier, watching a documentary about France v Israel and France v Bulgaria in 1993, the two defeats which ensured that Les Bleus didn't make it to the 1994 World Cup. We didn't want to go through that again. We would have a similar feeling before the final of the 2018 World Cup, when everyone in the squad remembered how much the Euro 2016 final had hurt us, and so we decided that losing was not an option.

In the period between the two matches, Didier Deschamps not only employed some psychological ruses, he also made some strong choices, replacing (the suspended) Laurent Koscielny (who was suspended), Éric Abidal, Samir Nasri, Olivier Giroud and Loïc Rémy with Karim Benzema, Yohan Cabaye, Mamadou Sakho, Mathieu Valbuena and Raphaël Varane. Later, in the weeks and months that followed, Samir would say that the players had complained about him and that they'd asked me to let the manager know so that he'd sideline him. He would call me one day, to get to the bottom of things, explaining that he didn't want his dreams of playing in a World Cup broken by an interpersonal issue within the team. But going to see the manager regarding a team pick is something I've never done, not for him, not for anyone. I have never gone to the manager to question a player's bona fides; it's not my role, even as captain, and it's not how a manager operates either. Didier sensed everything, saw everything and had no need of me to tell him what the dressing room thought. As regards everything else to do with the squad – aspects of play; the group spirit – yes, he did consult me regularly over the years, but regarding the choice of a player, never in a million years. That's what I told Samir.

As the return match drew near, we progressively felt a strength and a fervour rising within us. Noël Le Graët came to talk to us. The actor and comedian Jamel Debbouze came to screen the film *The Marchers* – based on the events surrounding the 1983 March for Equality and Against Racism. He spoke of what we represented and our country's values. It all counted, it all contributed to create a collective mindset favourable to the feat ahead of us. I spoke too, but everyone else also had things to say, and everything we said to each other over those three days, everything that we felt, guided us towards glory. We wanted the match to begin straight away, though it was only Sunday. Where the manager had been very clever was in succeeding in

A goalie's childhood, at Cedac de Cimiez.

With my grandfather, in my grandparents' apartment, which was my bolthole. Even then, Grandpa would tell his friends that one day his grandson would play for the French national team.

Above: One of my favourite photographs of me and my mum, who left us in 2008.

Right: I couldn't choose between football and tennis for a long time. This picture doesn't lie: I'm left-footed, but right-handed.

Below: Me, Sabrina, Gautier: the three Lloris siblings on Nice's pebble beach. I wish we'd spent more time together.

Right: Marine and I have built a wonderful family. Along with Anna-Rose, Giuliana and Léandro, we're living a new adventure in Los Angeles.

Below: Four generations of Lloris: me, my father and my son Léandro in the arms of my grandma, the rock of the family.

Leaping above the mêlée below, and William Gallas, in one of my greatest matches with Les Bleus: the World Cup playoff against Ireland in 2009, as Bacary Sagna looks on.

We didn't win any trophies with Tottenham, but I loved the years I spent at Spurs with Mauricio Pochettino. I've maintained a very strong friendship with him and the goalie trainer, Toni Jiménez.

My first time at the Stade de France, aged 19, with OGC Nice, in the final of the French League Cup, 2006, against Nancy (1–2). With Rod Fanni, David Bellion, Sammy Traoré, Jacques Abardonado, Olivier Echouafni (standing), Cédric Varrault, Marama Vahirua, Florent Balmont, Cyril Rool and Bakari Koné (crouching).

The World Cup goalies' club: with Steve Mandanda and Alphonse Areola, flanking Franck Raviot, who was always there for us. Our victories would have been nothing without the important role played by the staff, from the physios to the security officer, Momo Sanhadji, our confidant.

Above: Joël Bats was a role model and a mentor and remains a friend. I loved my Lyon years with him. He helped me as a goalie and as a man. I'm pretty sure we're not talking about football here.

Left: I spent more than 11 years in the French national team with our coach, Didier Deschamps. He was captain of the world champions in 1998, and I was his captain in 2018. This photograph reflects the kind of relationship he enjoyed with his players.

Without a doubt my most famous save, during France–Uruguay (2–0) in the quarter-final of the 2018 World Cup. I've often been given prints of this moment, taken from every angle.

9 July 2018, beneath the Moscow rain and swirling confetti, I had the joy of raising the World Cup first. The ultimate dream for any player.

Giuliana, the World Cup and Anna-Rose in my arms: a picture of joy, with Kylian Mbappé behind us.

getting into the heads of not just one or two players, but the entire squad. The day before the match, I said that we needed some craziness, but it wasn't the words which were important: it was looking each other in the eye and seeing hope there. In such moments you know who is who, and that you can all get somewhere together.

When it came to the match, we'd done enough talking. Pat Evra was wound up like a spring, Mamadou Sakho too, and as we stepped into a Stade de France packed to the rafters and quivering with energy – the flags, the singing, the fervour, the sense of a whole country behind us – we had the feeling we'd already won before setting foot on the pitch. So it goes with two-legged ties: first comes the despondency, then you say to yourself, 'Well, why not?'; hope gradually overtakes everything the closer you get to the match and, just before kick-off, you're sure you'll do it. On the pitch, there's a huge difference between a team which has nothing to lose and one which has everything to lose. When you've got nothing to lose, you're very dangerous, you become unplayable. When the Ukrainians walked onto the pitch that evening, amid the most wonderful atmosphere in the history of the Stade de France, having spent four days thinking they were virtually qualified for the World Cup in Brazil, not to mention being unbeaten for a year and not having conceded a single goal in eight matches; they didn't realize the scale of what awaited them.

This playoff match would mark a whole generation. Missing the World Cup in Brazil would have been a disaster for everyone. Didier Deschamps would have had difficulty getting over it, perhaps, and I, as captain, wouldn't have liked being the one who symbolized the failure. The match hit the Ukrainians like a hurricane: by the start of the second half they were reduced to ten men and trailing 2–0, thanks to goals from Mamadou Sakho and Karim Benzema. It was a boxing match, and our opponent never got off the ropes. In 2016 a survey by *France Football* ranked the match among the five greatest moments in the history of the French national team. Then Sakho pulled off the double, and I didn't have much to do at all except block a volley at 3–0 – and then we were free, amid a magnificent tumult, then the lap of honour, with Brazil on the horizon. It was insane. This crazy evening was what tipped us into a new and positive era, burying old demons, leaving Knysna and all the problems behind, and finally experiencing a moment of collective joy with our public. It was the foundation upon which the reconstruction of Les Bleus was built. Four of that evening's starting line-up (Paul Pogba, Blaise Matuidi, Varane and me, plus Giroud, who came off the bench) would be World Champions five years later, in 2018.

But Franck Ribéry wouldn't accompany us to Brazil. When he told us of his withdrawal, at Clairefontaine, we were rather taken aback because he was our major player, a popular figure in the squad and the leader in the eyes of the manager, with a real role of older brother, a role which he'd always hoped to have in the French national team and which he eventually got. It wasn't the same without him. I remember telling him – because we had a sense that something wasn't right – that there was more to his renouncement than simple back pain: 'Prepare yourself, Franck, we've got a Euro to win in two years.' I don't know what happened exactly. Everyone said that he felt French football hadn't got behind him sufficiently in the race to the Ballon d'Or. I regretted his absence because he really had a positive impact. He remained an exceptional player who made a difference and worked hard for the team.

I loved the World Cup in Brazil. For the country, for what it represents in the history of the game, as well as for the pleasure of experiencing a competition with players of my generation with whom I was very close. We had known each other since we were juniors together, and this World Cup, just like Euro 2016 two years later, will always have an emotional place in my heart, shared with lifelong friends of my own age. The age gap would be a little bigger in 2018, and I'm not even talking about 2022! Brazil was the last

BRAZIL!

World Cup where I listened to the same music as everyone else. We hung out together all the time, in each other's bedrooms, as well as the common areas.

We handled the first round very well. There was a 3–0 victory over Honduras – the first international match in history to use goalline technology – with a double from Karim Benzema, who got off to a great start. Next, a great match against Switzerland, whom we beat 5–2 after having led 5–0, even if I didn't appreciate our two conceded goals, notably the free-kick which passed below the wall. Nothing is trivial for a goalkeeper. In the third match, against Ecuador (0–0), the manager juggled his line-up and we discovered the Maracanã. Magical. In Rio the bus taking us to training would drive past Copacabana beach, with the giant screens and hordes of fans. We also had to sort out the rather tricky issue of accommodation for the families in Rio (although Marine hadn't come because Giuliana had just been born), and I had to convey our complaints, which wasn't my favourite aspect of the captaincy: the hotel wasn't suitable, the rooms weren't ready, the children couldn't go to bed, and the entire delegation ended up moving to another hotel, which led to some internal fallout in the FFF. This sapped a little of our energy, but it was before the Ecuador match, so had no impact on our preparation for the matches to come.

EARNING MY SPURS

Some friends had joined me in Rio. One day, after Ecuador, I called the lift in our beachside hotel to go down to eat. When the door opened I came face to face with Diego Maradona and his bodyguards: I didn't dare enter. I greeted him shyly, not knowing if he knew or recognized me; I could very well have been a common or garden fan wearing the strip of the French national team. After the meal, I went off to join my mates for a drink at the hotel bar, where we were joined by an Argentinian friend. Suddenly, who should arrive, but Maradona! I've rarely asked anyone for a picture, but this time I did, with all my friends and Diego, who remembered our meeting at the lift and had, in fact, recognized me. He talked to me about goalkeepers and seemed happy to have this picture taken with us. I still have that photo. It's a memory of a magical moment shared with my Niçois friends, who still talk about it, and a great souvenir for me too.

On the pitch, we won our round of 16 against Nigeria 2-0 at the very end of the match in the superb Garrincha stadium in Brasília. We also won the right to return to Rio and the Maracanã for the quarter-final against Germany, played at midday in scorching heat. My feeling about that 1-0 defeat is that we were evenly matched, so I couldn't reproach us for much. We were playing against a robust team typified by their talisman, goalkeeper Manuel Neuer.

BRAZIL!

Even though Karim's strike at the end of the match wasn't hard to block, Neuer was a wall. Qualification for the semi-finals came down to a duel won by Mats Hummels. But even though we'd been brought to a halt, I felt certain that this World Cup had opened up a new era.

You mustn't forget where we'd pulled ourselves back from, having very nearly missed qualification for the World Cup that past November. In June we yielded only in the quarter-final, to the future World Champions. With Euro 2016 at home very much in our sights, we were building up a force, and the French national team was finally popular again.

XIV

A Season in Hell

The evening of 13 November 2015, during the France–Germany match at the Stade de France, we heard the first explosion from the direction of the left-hand side of the pitch, round about where Patrice Evra was. I thought it was a large banger, such as you sometimes hear in stadiums in the South of France. The second explosion came a few minutes later. Returning to the dressing room at half-time, we still didn't know anything about the terrorist attacks. And since we didn't know, we played on. We learned of the horror when we got back to the dressing room at the end of the match. All the screens were showing reports of the murderous attacks in Paris, which had started with these two explosions at the Stade de France, where a man was killed on the esplanade.

We were asked not to leave the stadium. Very quickly we learned what had happened at the Bataclan, the massacre there and the deadly shootings at the café terraces. My brother was at the Stade de France. Many other brothers and sisters of my teammates were in Paris. Antoine Griezmann's sister, Maud, was at the Bataclan gig. There was a feeling of unreality, the bubble had burst, nothing made sense any more. The wait lasted ages. We stayed in the passageways for several hours, along with the German players, sharing the same anxiety, the same dread. I immediately called my brother from the dressing room, and I didn't feel relieved until I knew he was in a taxi. On that night of terror we returned to Clairefontaine around three in the morning. There we gathered in little groups in the bedrooms watching the TV news channels. Nobody wanted to be on their own.

We all needed to be with our families, but we spent the weekend at Clairefontaine, where it was easier to guarantee our security, wondering whether or not to play a friendly in England three days later. We decided to play out of principle, to respond to a night of horror with football, which had also been attacked, since the terrorists had aimed to get into the stadium. The images of the Bataclan haunted us all, but playing football was pretty much all we could do. We had to maintain this symbol of coexistence. All the Tottenham guys sent me touching messages, and when the evening came, in a Wembley decked out in blue, white and red, the English, solemn as they know how to be on grand occasions, sang an extremely moving rendition of 'La Marseillaise' with us, as the lyrics scrolled across the screen. At the press conference the day before the match, when the British journalists brought a floral wreath in homage to the victims, I didn't know what to say. I was there but not there, I felt empty. I knew that my words should be worthy of the emotional tenor of these times, of this cocktail of feelings, but it was hard to find the right ones. I tried to just say things plainly.

Those days left their mark on me. When Russia came to play the following month at the Stade de France, all the images came back. The trauma lasted a long time. It wasn't fear, just an overspill of emotions that covered the stadium. It took a while to get back to the way I felt before, the simple pleasure of being there and playing football, when the venue took us back to that night and our grief.

In the same month, November, the Valbuena–Benzema sex-tape affair broke – Benzema was under investigation for his involvement in a blackmailing ring trying to extort money from Valbuena. For efficiency's sake, the manager selected neither of them. At first, I thought it was just a bit of passing tension and that we wouldn't be going without a pair of such important players for very long. I was far from imagining that the affair would involve a formal complaint and a court ruling. I don't know what reply a captain can make to the press when their playmaker makes a formal complaint against the centre-forward. I couldn't take sides, I could only try to protect the team with measured language. Deep down, I asked myself the same questions as everyone else, and I wondered if their relationship could remain the same. But we very quickly understood that this affair would take on a national dimension, and that the recurring question of their absence, particularly Karim's, would continue for several years. It didn't make the manager's life any easier and it weakened the team. But we had no choice but to prepare for Euro 2016 in France with the squad we had. Football always forgets the absent in the end.

There were a lot of rumours going around about this affair. But, honestly, I still don't know what actually took place. Does the video exist? Who did what? I never had the slightest desire to stick my nose into it all. Everyone must be responsible for their own actions, and I didn't want to be responsible for those of others. I thought about the team and the upcoming Euros, and there was no question of letting this business plague me. It had happened at Clairefontaine in October and I'd not seen a thing. Nor had the others, that much I know.

I have never discussed this episode with either of the pair. I ran into Mathieu Valbuena with Tottenham, one evening in Athens for a Champions League match, and we greeted each other happily. I have never been one to get involved with something that doesn't concern me, even if it happened at Clairefontaine. I have never tried to find out who was guilty and who the victim was. I only know that it was a waste for them and for us, from both a sporting and a personal point of view. It doesn't correspond to the values we seek to promote. I don't think that Karim did anything against the squad, or that he sought to do anything bad to Mathieu. I think that he was a prisoner of his friendships, and was trying to sort out a situation that he didn't fully grasp.

Before Karim pulled on the blue strip again five and a half years later, I saw him in the Champions League, and then in Munich one summer during the Audi Cup. These were somewhat frosty reunions. I don't know if he hoped for a little more support from the other players. Perhaps he would have liked us to defend him and to pressure for his return to the team. But if we'd defended him publicly, him and only him, it would have been unfair to Mathieu. I have always had a different view of Karim: I played with him at Olympique Lyonnais, I really like him, and this situation distanced us. I was the captain of the team in which he was no longer allowed to play, but it wasn't the team's choice. Once the wheels of justice began turning, what could be done? And, anyway, the team still worked well without him. Up until the Euros, I had to talk about the affair at each and every press conference. I was accused of giving somewhat bland replies, but what really should I have said?

Just as we were experiencing a real popular enthusiasm around the Euros in France, Karim's interview with the Spanish sports daily, *AS*, in which he accused the manager of having given in to a racist chunk of the country, created a heavy atmosphere, for both team and coach. Deschamps' in-laws' house in Concarneau was tagged; those were a rough few weeks for him. The whole business hung over us up until our first match, against Romania. Once the Euros began, football became the only subject of conversation again.

We didn't have Karim, but we did have Dimitri Payet, who grew up on La Réunion. Dimitri was on fire, having just come out of a great season with West Ham, and it was he who carried us through the first matches. He was walking on water, and his magnificent goal against Romania in the last minutes kicked off Euro 2016. He was man-of-the-tournament as far as Les Bleus were concerned. On a personal level, this competition was the most enjoyable I'd ever experienced because I was with guys I'd known for ever and whom I was close to: Debuchy, Cabaye, Giroud, Koscielny, Costil, Jallet, Gignac, Payet, Griezmann, Schneiderlin and Sissoko. This was my generation, born between

1983 and 1987, and I retain a precious memory of our time spent together off the pitch. I wasn't to be found in my room much that summer.

Dimitri's goal against Romania didn't hugely affect our quality of play because we weren't yet tip-top, but his impact on the public passion and euphoria was enormous. He prevented us tumbling into concern and criticism. But even in winning the second match against Albania 2–0 we suffered. The manager had made some bold choices again, benching Antoine Griezmann and Paul Pogba, as in Brazil two years earlier. When they came on to play, it changed everything. The new arrangement with 24 teams had a strange impact: when you are top of your group and you play against a best third-placed team, one team is weaker than another, but has nothing to lose. That is why Portugal, who hadn't won a match, went all the way. It's why Côte d'Ivoire won the last Africa Cup of Nations. It's also why we messed up our first-half against underdogs Ireland, in Lyon, in the new stadium that Jean-Michel Aulas had commisssioned. A different Euros game began after half-time. After a first half where we didn't stop sliding about, I was less than polite: 'Fuck, guys, they're leading 1–0; we're playing a round of 16 in the Euros and you're incapable of picking the proper studs! Fuck!' Antoine moved into the centre and so the adventures of the wonderful offensive duo of Giroud and Griezmann began. They enabled us to kick it up a notch with each match: against Iceland in the quarter-final and Germany in the semi-final. It was only in the final where we fell short. We gave ourselves a scare against Ireland (2–1), but against Iceland (5–2), at a rainy Stade de France, on an ailing pitch, nothing could happen to us. Iceland had just dispatched England in Nice and we were ready for anything, notably their long throw-ins, but we respected them so much that we were done with them in 45 minutes (4–0), with Antoine serving up a goal and two assists, and Olivier two goals and an assist, amid a wonderful atmosphere. That day, our fans borrowed the Iceland fans' 'Viking' clapping.

The semi-final against Germany in Marseille will always be special. It's true that it wasn't my best match, and we suffered a lot, but Germany were the reigning world champions, the favourites. The din inside the Vélodrome was extraordinary, overwhelming, and filled us with insane energy. On the way from our seaside hotel to the stadium we felt an incredible power. We didn't need to warm up, we were ready to play. Everyone remembers Grizou's penalty against Neuer, several weeks after having missed one against him in the Champions League. It remains one of my greatest matches with Les Bleus. We were tough to play that evening: we all hung back and surged forward to fill the space as soon as we got a whiff of repossession. We had the legs, we had the heart, and even when they kept the ball from us, even when we felt we were resisting a steamroller, we were heroic. They played better, but we had the better mindset. I can see now the legs and expansive play of Blaise Matuidi and Moussa Sissoko, who was one of the best players in the Euros. It was truly something. It was also the first time in this tournament that the pressure was good for us. We had everything to win, in the end, and the French sportsperson always prefers having to conquer over being the favourite. Before the match, we told ourselves that we either win, or else we win. We won: 2-0.

The pressure was different in the final against Portugal, at the Stade de France. The fatigue too, since we'd had one day less recovery time than them. To truly mark your joining the French national team, you have to win a trophy. We had launched, we were soaring, we'd done all the necessary preparation, but success didn't come knocking. We had some opportunities, notably from Antoine, but they didn't lead anywhere. The Portuguese goalie Rui Patrício had a great match, and even when Cristiano Ronaldo was taken off injured in the 25th minute, we didn't for one second think that it would get any easier. He had just won the Champions League with Real Madrid, and although the Portuguese weren't playing particularly well, they had developed unbelievable mental toughness in the course of the competition. It all came down to two key moments, and a handful of centimetres. The first was Dédé Gignac's famous strike which grazed the post at the end of ordinary time. He so should have got that goal, old Dédé! He played for Tigres, in Mexico, and it was surely a wild hope that he would play in the Euros, but he fought for his place in the squad and was an extraordinary teammate, always the first to give the others a boost. This generous, football-mad chap deserved to be the hero of the final. He was just a couple of centimetres off. And so were we. I've long reflected on it, that ball which struck the post and bounced out instead of in. Winning the World Cup later overcame all that somewhat, but I still think about it often. It would have been a sort of culmination for my generation, the reward for an extraordinary joint adventure. It's the only way it should have ended. But that's sport for you. Portugal were fine winners, but it still hurts.

We were stunned by Eder's goal in extra time. It seemed to come out of nowhere. Just before that, Raphaël Guerreiro's free-kick had struck the crossbar. I was on it, but at maximum stretch and my knee struck the little metal bar which supports the side of the goal. I felt a piercing pain for a few seconds, but it was just the initial shock, and I remain convinced that it didn't affect my reaction to Eder's strike a few seconds later. I've had time to watch and rewatch the moment, to analyse it in depth. The pain didn't stop me extending to reach the ball. What made the difference was that fraction of a second where I didn't see the ball leave Eder's foot because Samuel Umtiti was blocking my view. The ball was going to pass to his right, and that made me lose a little bit of reaction time, that one little step to cover those few centimetres that I needed to make the clearance. The succession of circumstances was incredible, and the Portuguese victory amazing, from beginning to end. Lolo Koscielny, who had been given a yellow card in the 107th minute, couldn't risk committing any fouls to disrupt their play; Pat Evra was too far away to run back and cut off Eder on the inside; and although Sam Umtiti had chased him all the way, Eder outstripped him at the last moment and drove it into the corner. Every single detail was against us. At the start of the sequence, Guerreiro's free-kick, referee Mark Clattenburg had blown his whistle for a foul by Koscielny, giving him that yellow card – but the slow-motion replay clearly shows an Eder handball.

The remainder of the evening (and the summer) was painful. In the final minutes, we told ourselves that it wasn't possible, that it couldn't end like that. It hurt us deeply to see the Portuguese players raising the trophy in the Stade de France. I know full well that Ronaldo had experienced the same disappointment in the final of Euro 2004 in Lisbon, but we never imagined coming so far and halting on the verge of joy – in this final we'd been anticipating for over two years, after having undertaken such huge efforts with this squad of mates, and a whole country pushing us forwards during those magnificent days. Six years after Knysna, it was a positive performance, but the bitterness would linger for a long while. You turn the page because it's your job and the only way to stay competitive, but each time you turn round and look over your shoulder, you see this final lost by a few centimetres and you realize how close you came to being crowned in national glory, like the Platini generation in 1984, or the Zidane generation in 1998. The pain doesn't lessen with time. It returns less frequently, that's all.

Summer wasn't over. On 14 July (Bastille Day), I was in Corsica – Porto-Vecchio, to be precise – for the stag night of one of my best friends, Stéphane. At 11 p.m. all the phones in the restaurant began ringing. That's how we learned about the deadly truck attack on the Promenade des Anglais in Nice. I was on the phone with Marine for ages, and we were all the more shocked because my mother-in-law had suggested taking the girls down there to watch the fireworks. In the end she'd decided not to. I took the first plane back the next morning and joined the march organized by the mayor, Christian Estrosi. I wanted to be there. Nice is my city and we had been attacked. I often think about the families who lost loved ones. In that season of so many tragic events – the Paris attacks of the previous November, and this one in Nice – the Euros would have been a collective escape from reality, even though the Gendarmerie's elite tactical unit, the GIGN, were still on standby owing to the heightened threat of terrorism in the run-up to the tournament. The 14 July attack in Nice was a violent return to reality in all its horror. The city remains deeply marked by it, even today. There is a memorial, where we sometimes go to lay a wreath. When I drive past it, I can never forget. I know it's there. It'll always be the place where that happened.

XV

Slightly Mad

I'm convinced that you can't be a very good goalkeeper if you've been well behaved and calm your whole life. But I know too that most goalkeepers have a screw loose. With age, I've become better at hiding it on the pitch, which has enabled me to protect myself a little, and others too. At the start of my career, I was often reproached for my kamikaze attitude. People still remind me of one particular episode at Lyon, against Olympique de Marseille and their forward Baky Koné. I came out of goal to meet him on a long ball, made a screen with my body and slapped away the ball with my hand, but he couldn't stop in time and cannoned into me, striking me with his temple, as I recall. Unfortunately, he collapsed, having lost consciousness, and had to be taken off to hospital. I felt sorry for Baky, a lovely chap, with whom I had played previously at Nice. But the incident caused quite a fuss. When play resumed, Marseille's Boudewijn Zenden dragged his foot over me. I got up again, but said nothing. Then, at the end of half-time, as we came out of the dressing room to return to the pitch, all the Marseille players surrounded me. Laurent Spinosi, the OM goalie coach, a charming guy with whom I had always had good relations, kicked off and swore at me, to such an extent that I confronted him and everyone was scared that we would scrap. But it didn't unsettle me, and neither did José Anigo – then head of recruitment at Marseille – who yelled after me in the corridor: 'Hey, Lloris, it's not nice what you did, and to an old teammate, too!'

In France, it's no easy thing to be right against OM. So everything got blown up out of all proportion, and I can see myself now sitting in my car at Olympique Lyonnais' Tola Vologe training centre on the phone to RMC radio answering their questions, being suddenly forced to justify myself, when it was part of normal play and I was quite within my rights to go for the ball. I could understand the Marseillais' fear of losing their striker for a while and their wish to defend him. But why have such a go at me? Because I was an OL player? Because I was in competition with their keeper Steve Mandanda for the national number 1 jersey? I had the impression that loads of things came into it, but I had also decided not to play this game.

A goalie must command respect. When Fabien Barthez sent Ronaldo crashing to the ground in the 1998 World Cup final, nobody reproached him for rushing out of his goal. It even became one of the most famous images of the final. Fabien had acted magisterially. I have a tendency to head out of goal towards strikers, and sometimes it's rather borderline. But it's my game, my territory, my area, my responsibility. At Lyon Joël Bats liked to stimulate his goalies' craziness. Sometimes, in certain exercises, we had a forfeit. You had to rush out of goal and mix it up with the outfield players, tackle like crazy, win the ball and make a clearance – or else climb to the top of one of the club's buildings. He often took us out to eat at a fine restaurant, the Rotonde in Charbonnières, and when it came to dessert, we had to leap over the cheese dome. I've always had this little bit of craziness in me. Aged five or six, I loved diving headfirst into the strikers' legs. Even when you're calm and poised, you have to keep your craziness close at hand; it's key to our position as goalies and our decision-making. A keeper's reactions may sometimes appear excessive, but it happens that the wires spark and we lose control.

I prefer dashing out of goal headfirst into a player's boots rather than making a simple save. I love it when it's me or him. With VAR I've had to calm down a bit, but when I started out, I adored going to extremes. I have a lot of scars. Jamie Vardy lacerated my knee; a Crystal Palace striker cut open behind my ear; and there have been numerous stitches going back to childhood. Régis Bruneton, my trainer in the first level of juniors at Cedac de Cimiez, tells how one Wednesday morning, when he'd been challenging me in a series of shots on goal without managing to score, I wasn't able to finish the session after cutting my brow on the goalpost. As I was taken off to hospital, blood streaming from my head, I called out to him, 'See, Régis, you didn't score!'

Once, on a ski trip, my mother left me at skiing school for the week. I was ten, and one evening when she came to get me, she saw me busily involved in a ski-jump competition, tackling (with my helmet on), a huge mound that allowed you to soar for 15 metres. I loved all that, I was a go-getter. I'm calm in everyday life, but as soon as I step on the football pitch or partake in another activity, I need adrenaline and I just have to go for it. When I'm on holiday in the mountains with my children, I always promise myself not to ski, in accordance with my contracts. But it's not easy to keep your promises. I've always liked pushing the envelope, and that's how I ended up going too far, in Ibiza in summer 2015. It would cost me a wrist injury, which can only ever be bad for a goalie. I had gone on holiday with Stéphane, one of my best friends, who's just like me. In the little creeks, we began jumping from the rocks, then leaping from the cliff, higher up. We did a similar thing on quad bikes: first, a relaxed drive around the island with our wives, then an outing, just the pair of us, for speed and excitement. We spotted a hill. Getting up it was relatively easy, using our speed. Descending was the problem. I lost control entering a bend too fast and had the choice of flying into the ravine, which might well have been fatal, or hitting the rock wall. I chose the wall. Letting go of the quad bike, I fractured my triquetral, a bone in the wrist. Result: four to six weeks for it to reknit, at a time when my name was being mentioned in connection with Manchester United. I did two weeks of outfield-player training and only missed the opening match of the Premier League, against United, where I was on the bench. I think that the club was unaware of the origin of the injury, but not the manager. If Mauricio didn't give me a dressing down for the accident, then it was because I didn't tell him straight away. Originally, that Friday in Ibiza, I'd been told that I hadn't broken anything. Luckily, Stéphane is a physiotherapist and he drained the wrist, which had really swelled. But after an X-ray in Nice on the Tuesday, just to check, the diagnosis changed: fracture. I alerted the manager, but by then a week had passed between the accident and the diagnosis, which he didn't appreciate.

But although I am perhaps a little crazy, like all goalies, the flare-ups which have been caught on TV cameras are not further proof of it. At least, I think not. At OL there was one famous scene in the tunnel of the stadium at Nice. Having lost two points to Rennes in a 1–1 draw a week earlier (conceding a goal in the final minute), we were still on course for a top-three finish, leading Nice 0–2. I saved a penalty and then, towards the end of the match, we just totally lost control, giving away another penalty and picking up a red card before conceding another goal in the 92nd minute from an avoidable corner. In general, I know how to restrain myself, but that day, in the tunnel, where everything was filmed, it all came out and I screamed, 'I'm sick and tired of it! Sick and tired! We screwed up. You don't respect the club!' When I rewatch it, I don't like seeing myself behave like that. It's not pleasant. I've been told that it wasn't bad for my image, but, frankly, I would have preferred to avoid it. People saw me blow a fuse in Nice, but there were other episodes, not necessarily filmed, that's all. I remember one day when I abruptly interrupted the monologue of Lyon winger Michel Bastos, who was apologizing in the dressing room after a 2–0 defeat to Toulouse, when we ended the match with nine men.

The famous scene with my Tottenham teammate Sonny (Son Heung-min) had a more international audience, having been caught on camera for the Amazon series about the club. On 6 July 2020, against Everton, in a still empty stadium, we had another chance of making the Champions League; but we had suffered a 3–1 defeat away to Sheffield United four days earlier, a defeat which shook us up and which I was still smarting from. We were leading Everton 1–0 just before half-time when, on an Everton counterattack, Son continued running forward even though he could clearly see that we were going to lose possession and that he wouldn't have time to pull back. In three passes, Everton closed in on my area and fired off a strike which whizzed past the post. I immediately reproached him for his attitude rather heatedly, and he, surprised at me pointing the finger, insulted me back. When the ref blew his whistle for the interval, the argument really blew up. It wasn't even the insult which drove me mad, but his disdainful attitude when I spoke to him. That's how I lost control. In normal times, nobody would have heard us above the hubbub of the crowd. In the empty stadium, everyone did. What I blame myself for is not waiting until we returned to the dressing room to kick off. I don't know if we would have ended up physically fighting, but we would surely have shoved each other. It was Serge Aurier, a great character with a big heart, who held me back. Everyone watching the series heard my yelling when we entered the dressing room: 'It's the same for you, it's the same for Harry, it's the same for Lucas. The three up front should defend!' I was beside myself, and it lasted the whole of half-time. When José Mourinho addressed us, I was still hopping mad. I only calmed down when the game began again.

At the end of the match, it was all forgotten. Sonny and I adore each other – it's hard not to adore him – but sometimes he can get on your nerves, and there are aspects of the on-pitch battle which he has a harder time accepting. Amazon based almost all of their promotion of the series on this scene. I had been forewarned and I agreed to talk about the incident and to contextualize it. We didn't want to give the impression that football was all rosy, so I argued my point. Still, I prefer the outbursts which nobody saw. But I am sparing with them, which is essential if you want them to serve a useful purpose. There are players who want to talk all the time, and in the end they're just background noise. So you have to watch it. I'm not effusive, I say little, like Antoine Griezmann says little, but when he lets slip a few words at the right moment, as during the 2022 World Cup, it has an effect on everyone. These things come with time and maturity.

I've evolved as a captain and as a man. I wasn't ready at 25; but I was later. Experience allows you to anticipate things and sidestep stuff that might arise if you continue down a certain path. It generally avoids you getting angry afterwards.

XVI

The Pochettino Years

I loved playing at Tottenham, I loved working with Mauricio Pochettino, and I loved that feeling, so rare in football, of helping to build a club, of progressing each year without knowing our limits, and of sensing the extent to which a trophy at Spurs would be worth more than elsewhere. I regret not having won any silverware over my 12 years with the club – we often deserved to – but I don't regret staying there. When you win with a great historic club, it's the club which carries you. When you win with Tottenham, it's all of us – the manager, Harry Kane, me, the stalwarts – who carry the club.

The arrival of Mauricio and his staff in 2014 changed everything. At our first meeting, I told him that I remembered him, with his long hair, that I'd glimpsed him when he came to train with PSG at the Parc des Sports in Nice, the day before a match. I was immediately on board with his work ethic and his approach to the game. He wanted a highly aggressive, fierce team who would hold onto the ball and press forward. He considered that training sessions should be even more intense than matches. It was hard for some of the longstanding British members of the squad to switch software, so to speak. We would end that first season in fifth place, but it all made sense, the foundations were laid and Harry Kane was beginning to score. Kane's self-confidence and his way of claiming and assuming responsibility were already impressive despite his outwardly reserved and calm persona. In training, you would rarely see him do anything spectacular, and you couldn't imagine the monster of European football he would become.

To allocate the captaincy, Mauricio called together Younès Kaboul, Manu Adebayor and me, and told us: 'You're the three leaders, it's up to you now to decide which one will wear the armband. It's not my problem, but I'm counting on you.' Out of respect for his standing, we chose Younès as number 1, Ade as number 2 and me as number 3. But I would get the armband quite quickly owing to injuries and team compositions.

In the summer of 2015 it was rumoured in the press that my contract included a 35 million euro buyout clause. It wasn't true, I didn't have one, but I think the story was a means of sounding out the market. David de Gea was expected to go to Real Madrid on a transfer and I knew that Manchester United were interested in me. Pat Evra also told me about it at a get-together. But it wasn't something I was after. At Tottenham, I had finally found what I was looking for: consistent performance, managerial vision, a strong relationship with fans and good quality of everyday life. In the end, the question never arose because De Gea stayed where he was. As regards the next rumour sending me to PSG, it wasn't entirely false: then manager Jean-Louis Gasset had called Mauricio to suss out the lay of the land, and Mauricio told him that it was out of the question. He admitted it to me a little later.

In the second season with Mauricio (2015–16), the historic year that Leicester topped the Premier League, we would become a real force, with our third place the club's best ranking since 1990. Leicester's ascent was a magnificent thing, and since we were the ones who long believed we could prevent it, we ended up having to battle everyone.

Having spent 12 years at Tottenham, I know what I regret the most: the move from White Hart Lane. For our return to the Champions League in autumn 2016 we had to relocate to Wembley, as works began at our old stadium. Things would have gone completely differently at White

THE POCHETTINO YEARS

Hart Lane. We were unplayable there. That final season at the old ground, we remained unbeaten in all matches on that legendary turf (a first since the season of 1964–65), winning our last 14 matches of the championship! The place had an unbelievable energy, we mastered all the distances on the pitch perfectly, our positioning was tip-top and we could more easily grab the other side by the throat. I would have dearly loved to play in the Champions League at The Lane. In fact, I've always wondered how things would have gone if we'd stayed there. Many teams lost something when they left their ground. At the very moment when we felt capable of winning, we made life harder for ourselves by moving to Wembley for two years. We didn't do too badly (third, then fourth in the Premier League), but we started losing points at home which we never lost at White Hart Lane. For our opponents, playing at Wembley was like playing a final, whereas at White Hart Lane the question was only how many goals we'd slam past them. At the end of the 2016–17 season, we had 86 points, five points more than Leicester the previous year, but seven behind Chelsea. Still, there were no major regrets. Each year, we moved up a notch.

We stretched ourselves in matches, but above all in training. Mauricio was demanding and warm-hearted at the same time; pleasant to be around. Four times a year he invited players and staff to a get-together, which was important, particularly in a city like London where distances are a constraint. He brought a soul to the club that had been lacking there before. If I stayed so long, it's mainly because I was happy in this team, amid the fans singing my name in their blokey pronunciation: 'You-go! You-go!' I learned to get to know the club where, once a week, I ran into legendary goalie Pat Jennings, an icon for Franck Raviot (the goalie coach of the French national team) who felt privileged to be able to shake Pat's hand when he came to visit me one day. Pat still has his long hair and an elegant bearing. He was nearly 40 when he played in his one and only World Cup, with Northern Ireland in 1982, during which he reinforced his legendary status – the way he would come out of goal and seize aerial balls with one hand, often gloveless.

Daniel Levy, the chairman, is chillier than Jennings by nature, a hard-nosed businessman seeking to benefit from every situation. In 2018, after I won the World Cup with France, Daniel called me into his office: 'I'm happy for you, Hugo. I'd love to reward you for this. I'd love to give you a bonus. In return, you give me a unilateral option for a year's extension at the end of your contract.'

'Are you negotiating here, Daniel? I'm happy to, but then this is quite a different conversation.'

THE POCHETTINO YEARS

I gave him my figures that day and he never came back to me. But I never took it personally. It's business. You just have to know that there is always a quid pro quo with him.

In the 2017–18 Champions League we'd grown a head taller, but were still lacking in experience when we played in the round of 16 against Juventus. I took incredible pleasure in seeing our evolution. A captain's pleasure, too, in the face of such harmony. But it was at that precise point that the club should have accelerated our progression and supported our efforts by regenerating the squad. Summer 2018 typified this stasis when the club bought not a single player, at a time when Liverpool were snaffling up the best on the market. We were in front of them and they overtook us. The fans had placed an expectation on us to become English champions, but on wages much lower than those of our competitors – even certain West Ham or Everton players. We weren't playing on equal terms. It was inevitable in the end that the dynamic would crumble a little and the squad start to tire.

The 2018–19 season would be the one where we simultaneously progressed the furthest in the Champions League while finishing way behind Manchester City and Liverpool in the Premier League. In the championship, we were running out of steam, and we felt it as winter turned to spring. But there still remained the Champions League –

the miracle league – which might take us somewhere. In the group stage, we qualified after equalizing in the 85th minute against Barcelona (1–1) on the final day, and thanks to Inter Milan drawing 1–1 with PSV in the other match. That was the first miracle. Of course, in order to earn a little divine assistance, we'd had to help ourselves massively too. And, as always, the Champions League made me transcend myself. I felt invincible against Borussia Dortmund in the round of 16, particularly in the second leg.

Other miracles would follow. In early April, in the quarter-final first-leg against Manchester City (our first European match at our new ground), we conceded a penalty very early on in the game. With my back to the new stand, I faced off against Sergio Agüero. I had saved two penalties in January, one against Vardy and Leicester, the other against Aubameyang and Arsenal. Away goals still counted for tiebreaking purposes, so the penalty could blow this quarter-final for us. I knew Sergio well and that he could shoot crossways, dead-centre, anywhere. But I dived the right way and pushed the ball clear. I can still hear the roar which shook the stand behind me. Amazingly, I never conceded a goal to City in our new stadium.

After this 1–0 victory – thanks to a late goal by Son – came the second-leg match in Manchester, eight days later. It was another miracle and a match which people will remember for a long time. After having played nearly 900 professional matches, I know that nights like this can be counted on the fingers of one hand. Nothing was rational. I conceded four goals, nearly five, and yet I made saves: in other words, a horrible match for a goalie. Pure hell. But with full-time fast approaching, and City leading 4–2, Fernando Llorente came on and scored, turning this crazy night on its head again. I loved playing with him. He's an incredible guy, very positive, who adores football and human connections. At 4–3, City needed to score again to knock us out. And after six minutes of stoppage time, Raheem Sterling did so. The stadium exploded and Pep Guardiola ran around like a man possessed while we hung our heads in despair. It was the early days of VAR and nobody realized that Agüero had been offside. The referee disallowed the goal. I've never experienced such an intense emotional rollercoaster.

This *élan* and the feeling that a lucky star was watching over us didn't stop us completely messing up the semi-final first-leg against Ajax, losing 0–1. I have always found it hard to talk after defeats. Marine knows this, even if she says that it's been better these past few years. That evening, when I met up with her and some friends, I only broke my silence to say: 'It's over. When you can't even win at home . . .' I also had a hunch that an era was coming to an end. We were flagging. But the following week, when Liverpool, incredibly, turned the tables on Barcelona at Anfield (4–0, after having lost 3–0 at Camp Nou) the day before our second-leg match in Amsterdam, we were reminded how the craziest things can happen in the semi-finals of the Champions League.

In his pre-match chat, Mauricio tried to create an electroshock. Instead of his usual five- or ten-minute speech, he spoke for barely 30 seconds: 'This is *your* semi-final. This is *your* thing. You'll find the team line-up on the dressing-room board.' But at half-time of that semi-final second-leg, Ajax were leading us 2–0, that is to say 3–0 over both matches. We were fraught with tension. In our dressing room it was kicking off every which way: Harry Kane, frustrated at not playing, flew into a monstrous rage; I spoke, too; as well as the manager, of course. But, paradoxically, I sensed that the team was less impotent than in the first leg, and rather than shouting, I just kept telling them: 'One goal, guys, and it can change. One goal! We need to stay in the match.' And, indeed, a goal from Lucas in the 55th minute did change everything, because his second goal came just four minutes later. We could suddenly feel the fear in the other team. At 2–2 we were giving as good as we got. I had to make several more saves. Ours was usually a solid passing game, but that night we would qualify at the end of stoppage time as a result of a long ball from Moussa Sissoko that was nudged across the goalmouth by Llorente, then slotted home by Lucas for his hat-trick. The world's sports commentators screamed into their mics. It was surely one of the wildest moments of my career. Right before that goal, with the match being nearly over, I had moved up the pitch for a corner, but then had to run back down the whole length of the pitch at full speed so as not to leave my goal unattended – before running all the way back up it again (also at full pelt) to leap on Lucas and the others just in front of the stand containing the massed Spurs fans. The joyful images were something to see when we watched them later: Mauricio in tears on the pitch, then grabbing me in the mixed zone and not letting me go for anything in the world – euphoric, crazy with delight and unbelievably moved.

Less than a year after the World Cup final, I found myself in the Champions League final against Liverpool. In doing so, I became one of a very select band who had played in a Euros final, a World Cup final and then a Champions League final in succession. The day before the match, in Madrid, I ran into Dejan Lovren, the Reds' defender and my former teammate at Lyon. 'Hey, Hugo,' he called out. 'You got the World Cup, you can let me have the Champions League!'

I did not let him have it. It was snatched from us. The penalty awarded by referee Damir Skomina 24 seconds into the match – when the ball struck Moussa Sissoko's body and rebounded onto his hand – killed the final and wiped us out. From 2 June 2019, a change in the rules meant that a penalty would no longer follow if the ball struck a player's hand after touching another part of their body. The final took place on 1 June 2019, and something which wouldn't have been an offence the following day sealed the fate of the final before it had really begun. Liverpool contented themselves with putting on a robust defence. As for us, we could only try our luck and dare a little in our play during the last 20 minutes. It was not a great final. I played three finals with Tottenham – two League Cups (2015 and 2020) and one Champions League – in which we didn't score a single goal. It was so disappointing to have experienced all those emotions and for the adventure to come to an end in such a way. I don't know if everyone in the club and the team realized how difficult it is to reach a final, and how hard it is to come back from that. I'm not sure we understood that this was perhaps the only chance in our career to win the Champions League; that the club we played for was not one that was programmed to win it; that we could have avoided ever hearing again the complaint that Tottenham never won anything; that our names might have been engraved in the club's history forevermore. This is what that penalty took from us.

We do all have one engraved memory, though. Four days before the final, Daniel Levy called us all together to announce that, with the support of a sponsor, we would each receive a luxury aviator watch from the club. At first, we were excited to see the elegant boxes. Then we opened them and discovered that he'd had the back of each timepiece engraved with the player's name and '*Champions League Finalist 2019*'. 'Finalist.' Who does such a thing at a moment like this? I still haven't got over it, and I'm not alone. If we'd won, he wouldn't have asked for the watches back to have '*Winner*' engraved instead. I have considerable respect and esteem for the man and all he has done for the club as chairman – I got to know him – but there are things he is simply not sensitive to. As magnificent as the watch is, I have never worn it. I would have preferred there to be nothing on it. With an engraving like that, Levy couldn't have been surprised if we had been 1–0 down after a couple of minutes: so it was written.

At the post-match reception at the hotel, I had the impression that some people from the club and certain players were not sufficiently despondent at having lost. I would have liked people to come up to me and say, 'Don't worry, Hugo. Never again. We'll give you the means for a comeback.' But when I returned to my room on the night of the final, I think I had the same feeling as Mauricio and Harry: does the club really want to win? Real Madrid would never have celebrated a lost final, and we shouldn't have either.

Everything was hard after that, for Mauricio and for us. The club had finally invested in recruitment, but we hadn't got over the Champions League final, and the squad still wasn't sufficiently revived – and that's not to mention the tensions that would only grow following a decision by the club which would affect the team's day-to-day lives; a decision made without the consent of either the squad or the manager: to install cameras everywhere for Amazon's series about Spurs. In light of the sum mentioned – around ten million pounds – we wondered whether those whose season and activities would be affected, all those being asked to mic-up each day, would get a cut. The answer wasn't slow in coming: no.

So when the film crew placed little microphones on some of the canteen tables, we went and sat at other ones. We had to be careful all the time. The only place where we could speak freely was the training dressing room – we'd got them to agree that it would remain out of bounds.

THE POCHETTINO YEARS

Otherwise, they had mics and cameras everywhere – even at some practice sessions, which was no small matter: it was a constraint and it had consequences.

Football-wise, we suffered, conceding seven goals to Bayern Munich (7–2) in the following season's group stage of the Champions League, although they'd do one better in the quarter-final against Barça during lockdown (8–2). We were knocked out of the League Cup by League Two side Colchester United one evening when I was on the subs' bench. My son Léandro had been born four days earlier, the day before a 12.30 p.m. match at Leicester, and for the first time in my career I'd asked not to play, to not even come to the game. I didn't want to leave my daughters alone at home; I wanted to take them to meet their little brother the next day. Then, on 5 October 2019, in Brighton, I fractured my elbow during my first real involvement in the match. I was moving back on a ball that was descending very fast from very high when I decided to play it in two stages: to push the ball in front of the goalline to avoid me entering the goal with the ball, then grab it afterwards. Unfortunately, I slipped, fell backwards and my initial reflex was to brace myself against the floor with my two arms in order to immediately spring back into action. My left arm just went.

I don't know if it was simply bad luck – after the finals

of the Euros, the World Cup and the Champions League; the long seasons; the birth of my son; and the seven goals against Bayern (even if I wasn't at fault) – but the mental load may have had something to do with this injury, which would keep me off the pitch for three months. When it happened, I felt a pain shoot through me such as I'd never felt before. It was horrible. I felt my arm dislocate, separated into two parts connected by a thread. The pain was acute, unbearable, and the staff were unable to give me any gas to soothe it because the machine wasn't working. I suffered abominably until we got to the hospital, where they were able to reduce the dislocation of my elbow. Everything had torn – the muscles, the ligaments – but I chose not to have emergency surgery. My arm was huge, covered in oedemas of every colour: red, black, yellow. I made the right decision not to have surgery straight away because the swelling might have prevented me from recovering a normal range of movement. When I had surgery later, in London, the young chap who operated on me was used to working on boxers and rugby players; he grafted ligaments onto the bone and repaired the torn muscles. But he had to take out special insurance, never having operated on players with the kind of contracts that footballers have. It was the first surgery of my life and my first general anaesthetic.

I wasn't unhappy. Léandro was there and I was able to

spend a lot of time with him, which I hadn't been able to do with Anna-Rose and Giuliana. I really focused on the positives: the physiotherapy sessions with Dave, the Tottenham physio, who even came with me to Nice, and Christophe Geoffroy, the physio of the French national team, who spent five days in London. It would take a normal person one year to recover the full range of movement, with their arm extended, from such an injury; I managed this in ten days. I was only lacking five degrees, but they came back little by little.

During this time, Mauricio Pochettino called me at home one evening. He said that he was no longer the Spurs manager. I remember my answer: 'Quit fooling around.' He was insistent, as was I ('It's not true, I don't believe you.'), but I eventually got it. He left us a message on the dressing-room whiteboard, but it didn't stay there long. Some people took pictures of it because the ink could so easily be wiped away, and the gratitude too.

I hadn't seen it coming. After four seasons on the trot in the top four, it was normal to drop a few places in order to advance again with a fresh foot, and he should have had a little more credit in the bank. At the end of the day, it was Mauricio who'd created the expectations which had toppled him. I've sometimes wondered what I could have done if I hadn't been injured, and it hurt me not to have been able to help him, or the team, in my role as goalkeeper and captain day-to-day. The arrival of José Mourinho in his stead was the perfect plot twist for Amazon. José would allow them to poke their cameras and mics into every corner.

Since Mauricio lived ten minutes from the training centre, I went to see him very soon afterwards, and several times more. I wasn't the only one. It still astonishes me that he was removed when such a large proportion of the players were behind him, but there were also some guys he didn't wish to keep who extended their contracts as soon as he'd left. Maybe he also paid the price for the digs he made at the club in the media towards the end. He was surely just a victim of general attrition.

We didn't win anything with Mauricio, it's true. But it was a magnificent quest.

XVII

All the Gold in the World

It's not fair that there's such a huge gap between 'winner' and 'runner-up'. It just emphasizes the defeat. If there was a podium, with three teams and three medals, then second place would have greater value. At least the third-place playoff of a World Cup results in victory for a team. For the runner-up of Euro 2016, there was only defeat, which would take two years to get over.

I turned 30 in 2016. I hadn't felt the passage of time. But I was reaching those years where I had accumulated so much experience that I was able to approach the final stages of seasons and competitions knowing exactly what I needed to do and how to handle key moments. Whatever happened in a season, I knew I'd be ready. Time enables you to gain such self-knowledge. The French national team

ALL THE GOLD IN THE WORLD

was always the thread which ran through everything, and in a corner of my head was a space reserved for the next competition. I have fought throughout my career to preserve a certain level of consistency in club play so that I would be present and at my best when it counted. But with Les Bleus, the road to the 2018 World Cup in Russia didn't run so smoothly. People may remember my save from a Memphis Depay volley in the final minute of a match we won 1-0 against the Netherlands in October 2016, but nobody has forgotten my error in Sweden which led to a goal and our 2-1 defeat in June 2017. All keepers make mistakes, and we live with them, but I recall them with horror, particularly when they have an impact on the result.

I'd rushed my clearance because I saw 1-1 as a defeat, even though it wasn't the case, and the defeat came about from my error. I should have kicked the ball into touch, but, under pressure, I controlled then cleared it (badly) right up the middle, and Ola Toivonen intercepted it and scored from what must have been just over 50 yards away, in the last second of the last match of the season. I found it very hard to swallow. I waited all summer for September to roll around so that I could prove I was better than that. Later, Didier Deschamps asked me if I wouldn't have preferred to dive straight out and hug the ball to the ground, as I did at Tottenham. During the Pochettino era I was pretty much responsible for the restarts: when I received the ball, the two central defenders pulled back to the same line as me, while the wingers moved to the sides. At each pass back to me, I was conditioned: I knew that I could play under pressure, that I would find the solutions. But when you're playing for the national team and the ball comes to you, one player might take a position as in your club, but the other won't, and you find yourself without a solution but under pressure because you've stopped the ball and the other team's pressing you.

We all need criticism. It stings, but it feeds the thirst for performance and the desire to prove yourself. That's not what I think in the heat of the moment, of course. Rather, I think: 'Let them all go to hell. You'll see, in the next match ...' For the Sweden match, I deserved it. But I've sometimes been reproached for ridiculous things that betray an ignorance of the goalkeeper's job by those making the judgement. And sometimes the praise is as unjustified as the criticism. Then there's the debate regarding a goalie's footwork, when the very essence of the position is stopping the ball. People lose all perspective. In an interview, the Italian defender Giorgio Chiellini reproached Pep Guardiola for having made re-starts the prime function of defenders. It's rather similar for goalies, although I note that Guardiola did win the Champions League in the end (with Manchester City in 2023) playing four central defenders.

I sometimes read the newspapers, as well as *L'Équipe*, but after the Sweden match I didn't need to read anything at all to know that I was guilty. In such situations I raise my hand and say, 'My fault.' After this match, I shouldered my responsibilities until the end of qualification. People have told me sometimes that I've been at a disadvantage in the media because I don't have an agent, who would have pushed me and maintained a network of contacts. Firstly, players who do are neither aware of nor responsible for such things. Secondly, that would have been a very bad reason to take on an agent.

In September, we drew 0–0 against Luxembourg, and the goalie had nothing to do with it. But we won in Bulgaria, drawing on a collective strength in a febrile stadium, and ended up qualifying for the 2018 World Cup. The youngsters – Kylian Mbappé, Ousmane Dembélé and Thomas Lemar – had just arrived in the squad. Kylian was a kid when he showed up, all of 12 years younger than me. I recall Lolo Koscielny and myself sighing at the end of an opposed practice session: 'They're like planes. They go much too fast.' And we were far from imagining what Kylian would become.

It would be an exaggeration, untrue even, to state that

our preparations for the 2018 World Cup ran completely smoothly. Didier Deschamps' suitability as manager was questioned, notably by certain former world champions of 1998. Everyone was hauled over the coals, whether it was Olivier Giroud, Antoine Griezmann or me. Didier didn't have his team yet, and Blaise Matuidi and I had a discussion with him in Lyon during practice, after the France–USA friendly had finished 1–1. I'd been singled out because I'd conceded a goal from a ball which slipped between me and the near post, but nobody considered the fact that the strike had been deflected by Djibril Sidibé. I know how to prepare for a final stage – I know myself – yet I was being judged as if the World Cup had already started. I knew that it wasn't the moment yet. I was a little offended by Didier's words to me –'Hugo, you've had periods where you were a little more successful' – to which I replied that my problem was a collective one. I explained that I didn't like the feeling I was getting from the team: 'I'm sensing some bad group vibes. I feel that we're fragile, that we're getting penetrated in midfield, that the defensive line is not doing enough upfield, or not doing it well enough, and that we're very young. As for me, you don't have to worry – I know where I'm going – but if we continue like this, we're going to get slaughtered in midfield.' He reacted in his usual manner: listening, but without explicitly agreeing. That's how he works. He collects your opinion and you find out later if he took it on board.

For the first match in the competition, against Australia, Didier again made his decisions according to his convictions. We won 2-1, but it was tough going, and the debrief the next day was carnage. I'd never seen Deschamps like that. The much-shared clip, where you see him cross with us, was without a doubt the calmest and kindest he was in that meeting. This was the only time in my career in blue when I saw the manager go over a match with video footage, backed up with stats of who ran furthest and at what intensity, pointing at a different player each time and yelling his criticisms. That's where our 2018 World Cup started. It's where the penny dropped. We had to win that first match, but this reappraisal of our performances was essential. We had so many fast players that the coach was tempted to start them all. But sprinters are not made for endurance; they need to recover after their high-intensity sprints. And with three players like that, we'd have been in great difficulty when falling back defensively. So the coach adjusted the midfield before the second match, against Peru (1-0), placing Blaise Matuidi on the left wing. We were criticized yet more, but on the evening of my 100th cap we knew we could go places. We felt strong like that, a super-solid team that ran, that adapted to the opponent; a killer team you couldn't let seize even a bit of room.

With us already qualified for the next round, I didn't play the third match against Denmark, in which nothing happened because a 0–0 draw suited everyone. But I was at peace. Before Australia, I read that I had 'much to prove'. One save later – as well as several sallies from goal on aerial balls – I was 'unfazed; there when I needed to be'. What were they imagining?

From our base in Istra Forest, north of Moscow, we felt a collective force growing. This squad had a soul, with a mixture of generations accepted by the veterans and confirmed players. It was the first time there was such an age gap between the young players and me. To the strength we had at Euro 2016, we added the freshness and wildness of youth, starting with Kylian, who would change so many things.

On the horizon of the round of 16 were Argentina and Leo Messi. At the meeting to go through the starting line-up, the manager outlined his plan on the blackboard. Having explained our roles when we didn't have the ball, Antoine Griezmann interrupted him: 'We're going to close down the space, pull back to the penalty area and I'll mark the number 6.' The coach looked at him, eyes wide, in awe of the sacrifice this would require of a striker. Antoine insisted: 'I do it at Atlético, no problem. I'll take care of it.' And that's how we played against Argentina: Olivier handled the two centre-forwards and Antoine pulled back like a midfielder to mark Javier Mascherano, which enabled two players to mark Leo, so supporting N'Golo Kanté, who stuck to him like glue. It's the tactic we'd follow all the way through. Even Paul Pogba would be transformed. People reproached us for not playmaking, but we were a truly competitive team. You'd have to get up early to beat us. And even that wouldn't have sufficed.

France 4 Argentina 3 was an exceptional match. After leading 1–0 we stuttered at the start of the second half, somewhat stunned when the Argentinians managed to get in front 2–1, but Benjamin Pavard's goal changed everything. 'Why are you even attempting a shot?' I half-thought to myself, from my end of the pitch. But seen from behind, the trajectory was even more unbelievable. Then the sky fell on Argentina's heads as we scored two goals in four minutes. Agüero's header to make it 4–3 in stoppage time came from the only sequence where we'd given Leo Messi enough time to breathe. The Argentinians had another opportunity afterwards, but when you become world champions you forget the handful of centimetres which might have tipped things one way or the other.

That day, we all thought that Lionel Messi would never

win a World Cup. He had lost the previous final, he was losing this round of 16, and I could see at the end that he was simply dazed. You could read the pain in his face. At that moment, I'm not sure if he still believed in his chances of becoming world champion one day. It's because of such moments that I'm opposed to the idea of holding the World Cup every two years. It's the four-year interval, the long wait, which makes it special, magical. You can't make it commonplace. It has to be so that, aged 30, a player can't know if he'll be able to play another one, let alone win it someday.

We had six days to prepare for the quarter-final against Uruguay, which enabled us to spend a lot of time together. We needed to decompress; even pull the pin out of a fire extinguisher, as Adil Rami did, on a night that has gone down in posterity.

Arriving at the gym every morning, I would run into Adil: 'Hugo, I can't take it any more. I need a day off. Can't you go talk to the coach and get us a day off? We could see a bit of the place.' I could understand his desire to have a nosey around, but if he'd sneaked out in Istra he would have had a high chance of coming face to face with a bear. This being the World Cup, a day off was a queer idea, but after discussion with the staff and manager, a dinner was agreed. We hired out a whole restaurant on a boat, looked at the wine list (a touch of France, this far from home) and got back to the hotel in a somewhat festive mood, noisy too. The youngsters tried to get into Adil's room to tip his bed over. At which point Adil grabbed the extinguisher and filled the corridor with foam and fumes. We were wondering how to cover ourselves without smothering ourselves when the alarm went off and we had to evacuate in the middle of the night. Outside, beneath the stars, we remained united in our tomfoolery. We sensed that the manager was angry with us, but when he got his phone out at one point and earnestly engaged in conversation, I suspected that there was no one on the other end, that he was just pretending. He must have sensed that something was happening with the squad and that this moment shouldn't be lost, that it was helping unify us. Standing outside in the forest air at two in the morning, I was already preparing our arguments in expectation of a rollicking, but when the alarm stopped we all went back to bed and the coach said nothing. At lunch the next day Adil stood up, apologized to everyone, and that was that. Several months later Adil gave us each an extinguisher engraved with our name and the number of the shirt we wore at the World Cup. Real class. It was a pivotal moment in our adventure.

The quarter-final against Uruguay arrived, but without Edinson Cavani, which was a good thing for us. In Nizhny

Novgorod each team had their chance. We opened the scoring from a free-kick from Antoine and a header from Raphaël Varane, and I had that famous save to make just before half-time. The second half was more complicated, but we scored from a long strike (Antoine, again) thanks to an error from the Uruguayan goalie, Fernando Muslera. I would later learn that he had lost two people close to him a few days earlier. He and I don't know each other, but we have a historic relationship: our respective World Cup careers commenced in the opening match of the 2010 edition, and he's a goalie I've always appreciated. His error allowed us to free ourselves and slip into the semi-finals.

So, that save. I have many photos of it. People often give me framed prints, taken at the moment when I'm horizontal, one metre above the ground. But, for me, what's powerful is what you don't see: the three steps to reposition myself at speed closer to my line and, on Martín Cáceres' header, that little step which allowed me to dive quite far to smack the ball clear with a firm hand. I couldn't push it to the side for fear of it rebounding onto me or into the goal, so I slapped it forwards a little. But I was able to perform the second movement (I've always been known for responding fast and getting up quickly) so well that after the save I already knew that I had to immediately be ready to spring forwards to meet Diego Godín, block the goal and force him to put the ball over it. When it comes to saves, you always need to see beyond the photo, even when it's a fine one. Everyone notices how beautiful Roger Federer's backhand is, but almost no one understands that the reason for it is because he moves faster than other players. When you see a keeper come out of goal on an aerial ball, you have to break down their movement from beginning to end: if a goalie makes two little steps to adjust their position, it'll be an easy save; whereas if they don't, they'll have to make a spectacular one, which will surely be more attention-grabbing. When a goalie knows to take one more step so he doesn't need to dive, it makes a real difference, but virtually nobody notices.

I've often been asked to list my own top-five saves, the way strikers are asked for their top-five goals. This was definitely one of them because of the importance of the match, among other things. Sometimes you achieve the required repositioning, but you don't have the proper timing to dive, so you arrive where the ball is, only to watch it fly past you. With this save, when you break it down in its entirety, you realize that the timing was perfect from start to finish.

For my four remaining saves, I'm going to pick one for each strip I've worn, since I've loved them all. With Tottenham, the most spectacular save came at Bayer Leverkusen in the group stage of the Champions League in 2016–17. Chicharito (Javier Hernández) had a virtually empty goal before him, leaving me the most infinitesimal chance of preventing him from scoring. I managed to get a firm hand on the ball, then hold it in that hand while doing a roll on the line, before getting up as if nothing had happened – as the whole stadium and the Leverkusen players screamed for a goal. But I knew that the ball hadn't crossed the line; I'd made sure I knew where I was in relation to it. And goalline technology confirmed this. It was the roll with the ball in one hand that left an impression.

With Olympique Lyonnais I'd pick that save from the Wendel header at the end of the second-leg quarter-final match of the Champions League in 2010 against Bordeaux. There were others, but this one was symbolic, coming at a crucial moment in the match when it could have been curtains for us, amid a torrid atmosphere, at a point when the club had never qualified for the semi-finals of the Champions League. The ball ended up not that far from me, which gave me the time to intervene, but I had to keep a firm hand and push it away to the side.

The thing is, I don't want to include in my top-five any spectacular save that didn't have a powerful context. And there was certainly context to my chosen save in the strip of OGC Nice. This came after the injury to my left knee in the 2007–08 season, which scuppered me twice and resulted in the club chairman, Maurice Cohen, lending me his Smart car because I didn't have an automatic at the time. I had returned to the first team too quickly, fallen again, then was put in the reserves that competed in the fourth tier, in order to ease me back into things, before once again returning to frontline play against PSG in a match screened live on Canal+. David N'Gog headed the ball after a Jérôme Rothen free-kick, it rose, headed for the goal, and to clear it I leapt like an uncoiled spring. Commenting on the goal with sports journalist Grégoire Margotton was my future France coach Didier Deschamps, who had analysed the sequence: 'It's fabulous! Lloris just flies through the air! It's not an easy one, he pushes it well; you can see how explosive a reaction he has. The ball's far from him and he manages to clear it with a firm hand.' Even back then, Didier was precise and to the point. I was 19 and I'd just come back from an injury: it's the very context of this save that makes it such a strong memory for me.

With Les Bleus, there's another one I can pick, from a World Cup qualifying match against Bosnia in March 2021, on a header which rebounded right in front of me: I managed to get the ball to pass over the woodwork. It wasn't a simple save, but I like it when there's a story behind it. And the story was much more striking against Uruguay, in Russia. Everything came together and our tight-knit squad progressed.

In the semi-final, we guessed that Belgium would be the strongest team we'd have to play. The Belgians had just knocked Brazil out and they'd been playing together a long time, with their 3-4-3 that was so gruelling to play against, and Eden Hazard at the peak of his craft, alongside physical players such as Romelu Lukaku and Marouane Fellaini. They were capable of threatening us in the air, in the spaces, one-on-one – everywhere. They had no flaws, except for their right corridor, perhaps.

Much had been said about the set-plays and corners before the match, and that's where we got them, on a corner from Antoine and a header from Samuel Umtiti. Me, I had a clearance to make from a Fellaini header, which put me in the match, and there were other important saves. But what counted, too, was staying calm and making sure the team knew it.

I'm aware of the Belgian debate surrounding our 1-0 victory. But when you rewatch the match, you notice that we had numerous occasions to make it 2-0, and that their goalie, Thibaut Courtois, made two or three saves, including one from a Corentin Tolisso strike. What's true is that we never sought to play beautiful football, so close to our ultimate goal. We wanted to be strong, impossible to play, impossible to shift, and to stay in Russia till the end. As Paul Pogba said: 'I want to continue eating pasta; I don't feel like going home!' This qualification for the final of the World Cup was a magnificent moment of collective joy. It continued when we got back to Istra, our 'home' in the forest. When you feel good in a squad, you get attached to places, you like getting back to base camp knowing that the adventure continues. We stretched the time out by staying together a lot, sometimes around a camp fire, chatting about anything and everything – not necessarily the World Cup.

We were in the World Cup final. Everyone came: my grandma, my dad, Gautier, my sister, Marine, my daughters, friends. But our preparation was completely different compared to how we had approached the Euro 2016 final. Two years earlier, things had taken an emotional tack. The manager screened a moving film about our families. This time, we were cold and hard. In our attitude, there was something of the, 'It's ours: we're going to win it.'

As we set out for Moscow, the day before the final, the assistant manager Guy Stéphan stopped me just as I was boarding the coach. 'You OK, Hugo?'

'Yes . . .'

'You've done a little weightlifting, right?'

'What?'

'Yeah, to prepare yourself . . .' And, laughing, he mimed the movement of a player raising a trophy several times.

But although we felt this strength, we couldn't forget what had happened two years earlier against Portugal. Croatia were really a very fine team with some great players. We approached this final forgetting that we were the favourites, forgetting the billion TV viewers. Indeed, when I went to warm up, there were only two fans I looked for: my two daughters, whom I hadn't seen for 40 days. I watched them even as I went through my drills. They waved back at me. We prepared for this final down to the smallest detail, even finishing our warm-up inside because of the pre-match ceremony. Everyone in the team said a few words: I did; Raph Varane did; the manager did, of course; and Paul Pogba made a long speech because he needed to. The things you say in such moments are rarely original. You stick to the good old basics. Despite all that, we completely blew the first half: they pushed us about and shook us up, but we found ourselves leading 2–1 without having had a single shot on goal. After Mario Mandžukić's own goal, the Croatians came back into the match with an Ivan Perišic strike deflected by Raph. But following my quickly taken long goalkick towards Kylian, he got a corner which resulted in Antoine's penalty. At half-time we practically felt like we did after our first match against Australia: we

ALL THE GOLD IN THE WORLD

were leading but the manager gave us a right ticking-off because we'd allowed ourselves to be eaten alive. In the second half we played off our speed, but the Croatians had the ball and I made a save at 2–1 in front of Ante Rebic, before we got ourselves together and carved out a cruel, definitive advantage with Paul's and Kylian's goals, to lead 4–1 and feel, for the first time, that we had the World Cup in our hands.

The whole stadium felt it was over, even though there was half an hour left. It was strange. There was a palpable feeling in the air, of a tension now slackened off. But that was no excuse for my error, which enabled Croatia to pull back to 4–2. After a throw-in for us, Sam Umtiti ran the ball back to me down the left wing. I controlled it and waited for the others to move; but rather than kick the ball into touch over Mandžukić's head, or towards Raph who had a Croatian player too close to him, 25 metres from me, I tried to sidestep the striker, which was not the right solution. In a different context I'd have played it into touch, but at 4–1 I no doubt gave in to the general ambiance too. I always prefer my saves to have impacts and for my errors not to. And this error had no impact. Just before the final whistle, I came out of goal to grab an aerial ball. Getting up, I knew that we were champions of the world.

How to describe what happened next: the joy, the euphoria,

the shouts, the running about all over the place? That Sunday night we became kids again, yelling with delight in the school playground. It was just a bigger playground, that's all, and the joy would be for ever. I can see the goalies dashing towards me: Steve Mandanda and Alphonse Areola, with Franck Raviot. A bit like in films, the images flashed past in my head; I thought about my career, and it all came back – the pain, the long slog, the sacrifices, the pride, the recognition – as if you had to reach the end of the story to be able to look back from the start.

I can see Didier now holding me back, just before mounting the podium to receive the World Cup, whispering, 'Savour this moment, Hugo. Take the time to raise it, this trophy.' At first, I didn't really understand what he wanted to say, but I understood later. We had to make this moment last because it would pass in the blink of an eye and nothing would ever top it. When I lifted the World Cup, I felt the weight of history, of what it represented, and the lineage we were now a part of, all of us together. On the walls of our hotel in Istra were photos of previous captains brandishing the World Cup: Maradona in 1986; Lothar Matthäus in 1990; our coach in 1998; Fabio Cannavaro in 2006; Iker Casillas in 2010; and Philipp Lahm in 2014. So as the first of us to touch the trophy, I felt an immense pride as I raised it aloft.

The next instant, the storm broke, and there was that

ALL THE GOLD IN THE WORLD

moment, beneath the pelting rain and the confetti swirling about us in the Moscow air, when I went to get my girls so that I could hold three precious things in my arms: Anna-Rose, Giuliana and the World Cup. I have a cherished photo of it, and another similar picture with Kylian in the background, and it's a photograph that my girls love. All this joy concentrated into those magic minutes before the cruellest moment of the evening: the anti-doping control, which took N'Golo Kanté and me away from the celebrations for close to an hour. There you are in a quiet room far from everything and everyone, a medal around your neck, champion of the world, without even a nice cool beer to make the minutes pass. I'm still angry with FIFA, even today. They stole the most important hour of this World Cup from me. When we eventually got back to the dressing room, the exhilaration was still there, but I'll always miss not having experienced the most euphoric, the most primal emotions. I'll never get that hour back that they took from me. It still hurts. Luckily, no one took the night that followed, nor the one after that, nor several more; neither could they take that certainty, as the coach would tell us, that we were world champions for ever, bound by an unbreakable bond.

XVIII

A Lesson

I can't limit this book to the moments of pride, or focus solely on the cut and thrust of matches won and lost. Out of honesty, and because I learned a lesson that could be instructive to others, I must discuss an episode off the pitch which didn't paint me in a very good light, and which earned me an early morning greeting from a horde of paparazzi outside my home when they learned of my arrest in central London the night of 23–24 August 2018.

Laurent Koscielny, Olivier Giroud and I had decided to have a good night out at a restaurant in London's West End, as we sometimes did. We hung out regularly when the pair were at Arsenal, and we spent a lot of time together with each other's families too. The idea was also to lift Lolo's spirits, after he'd been left out of the World Cup because of injury.

In November 2017 Lolo had announced that he'd retire

A LESSON

from international football after the 2018 World Cup. I remember thinking that all those who'd announced such a decision a long time in advance had made things complicated for themselves because an announcement like that created a sort of pressure. It's also why I protected myself before the 2022 World Cup, postponing the decision on my retirement until the end of the competition, and refusing to discuss the caps record. Lolo found it very hard to get over the double whammy of rupturing his Achilles tendon in May and of a World Cup victory without him. It's quite understandable, and I feel that he displayed a rare honesty in admitting his disappointment, when it would have been so easy to say that he was happy for the others and that he felt like he was a bit of a world champion too. When it comes to the objective of an entire life, feelings are obviously rather more complex. I think that the six players left out of the 1998 World Cup squad at the last moment (Nicolas Anelka, Lionel Letizi, Ibrahim Ba, Martin Djetou, Pierre Laigle and Sabri Lamouchi) all found it very hard to stomach – except Anelka, perhaps, because he was very young. He was the only one of them to play in a later World Cup, in 2010, even though he maybe regretted it. The others never got over it. Being world champion changes your life, and I never resented Lolo for admitting that he would have preferred for the World Cup not to have had such a beautiful ending without him. Nobody could stand in his shoes, and it was easy to comprehend that the further we progressed in the competition, the more it pained him to be missing it. The evening of the final in Moscow, Lolo came to see me at the anti-doping control (the FFF had invited him to the competition), and he tried to be happy for us, but a bit later he admitted, with remarkable sincerity, the extent to which he had become increasingly inconsolable, as match followed match.

After an interview with *L'Équipe* in Hampstead on the Friday afternoon, I ordered a car to go pick up Lolo at home first, then head into town where we would meet Olivier. But the driver cancelled the ride at the last moment, so I took my own car in the end. We spent our evening at a French restaurant, where a merry time was had. The three of us were hardly going to share a single bottle of wine – it's not done. But what with two of us being world champions, the other restaurant patrons bought us tequila shots after our dessert. You accept out of politeness at first, but then it never ends. It must have been around one in the morning when we decided to leave the place. I didn't want to get home too late, even though the next day's training session, two days before the match against Manchester United, was more of a pick 'n' mix (warm-up, rondo, then back to the dressing room). We'd planned on having dinner, a couple

A LESSON

of glasses of wine, then home to bed, no consumption of spirits. When I got behind the wheel of my car (a very bad idea) outside the restaurant in Mayfair with Lolo, we were, let's be honest, somewhat tired. Later, in a 'Yes/No' segment for *Téléfoot*, Olivier answered, 'Yes,' to the question 'Would you have been over the limit if you'd been arrested instead of Hugo?'

We'd barely passed the first junction when I heard the police siren. I stopped the car and the policeman asked me to roll down my window: 'You were driving rather slowly and you've just gone through the lights on amber.' I told him that I was sorry, and when he said he'd have to breathalyze me, I thought it best I come clean: 'Look, I'll be honest with you: I've had a few drinks.' But his reaction was most abrupt. He ordered me out, pressed me against the car and handcuffed me. Then he told Lolo to exit the car and go home, which caught him off-guard, given his state. The policeman then parked my car.

Under the effect of the stress, I relieved myself of a considerable pressure in my belly, before one of the two policemen put me into their car to take me to the station. There, I went through the whole booking rigmarole – photos, fingerprints, and so on – and as they were leading me to the cell where I would spend the night, I had the presence of mind to remember the next day's practice session and to request my authorised phone call so I could inform the manager.

Alone in my cell, I managed to sleep a little on the very stiff bench – the evening's shenanigans no doubt aiding slumber. They released me in the morning, called a taxi for me and gave me back my phone. Lolo's wife had already called Marine at three in the morning to let her know, so the first thing I did was reassure her: 'I got myself arrested. I drank a bit and failed the breathalyzer test, but everything's fine, there wasn't an accident.' Marine told me that the paparazzi were waiting in front of the house. It was the cleaning lady who'd warned her. They'd rung the bell. When I got there, I saw the guys from the *Sun* and told the taxi driver to carry straight on. I stepped out a little way away and opened the gate remotely so as to get in faster. I refused to answer their questions, and when they tried to follow me in I reminded them that this was private property. They camped outside for three days, and were still there on the Sunday morning when I left to go to training, where I apologized to the whole squad. I knew I'd be in for a rough few days. There was a whole debate in the British press: can Lloris remain as captain? The manager asked me for an explanation and I told him what exactly had happened. He also wanted to know how I was feeling before the next day's match against Manchester

A LESSON

United at Old Trafford, and I assured him that there was no problem, that he could count on me. The club wanted me to put out a message on social media, and I apologized again. Part of me didn't want to apologize publicly for something that was a private matter, but another part of me remembered that drunk driving is a major issue, particularly in Britain, that I was captain of Tottenham and that I should apologize out of principle, not least because I was living in Britain, and you can't only set an example when it concerns easy things. I eventually apologized out of conviction, because I had to take responsibility for this mistake, because it could be an important lesson for many, and because by missing a practice session two days before a match, I couldn't completely separate my private life from my life as a footballer.

I don't regret my evening out, but I infinitely regret trying to drive home, of course. It was a concatenation of circumstances because I'm not a party hound – I go out like that maybe three or four times a year. But I've sometimes wondered why I was stopped when I was driving slowly but not badly, and I've even wondered about the restaurant's responsibility in letting me leave, and the other times this could have happened.

There was a before and an after. It has never happened to me again. I downloaded all the taxi and ride-hailing apps and I stopped taking the car to drive into central London. This was a rough episode for me and my family. When Marine and the children came back from Nice we went for a walk on Hampstead Heath and the paparazzi were still following us. I found it unbearable that I had created this situation when I had spent my life trying to protect my family. I felt terrible about exposing them to this.

On the Monday night I played a stupendous match at Old Trafford. Mauricio had kept my inclusion in the line-up a secret until the last moment. The club wanted to punish me, but he refused. When they learned the size of the fine I had to pay (£50,000), they must have concluded that it was sufficient, but one of the club's sponsors chose to remove me from its posters. I picked up an injury not long afterwards, and when I returned I sensed that the media (even the sports outlets) looked at me differently for the first few months and remained judgemental. It wasn't the case in France, where this story would have had a human pull bringing me closer to the public, but I was living in Britain. A world champion who spends the night in jail was a great story for the tabloid press, which published my address and the value of my house, even though I rented it. It was our family bolthole and we wondered if we should move or not. We did in the end, but not because of that – our neighbour, a Russian, was having extensive

A LESSON

building work undertaken, but he had all his assets seized and couldn't complete the work.

I experienced the shame of a public trial. When I arrived at court, close to Marylebone Station, a pack of around 30 journalists were waiting. They jostled me as I got out of the car, asking me questions I was never going to answer. After the sentencing, which was a relief (20-month suspension of my licence plus the fine), I found myself again being jostled by the press, and I swore to myself that I would make sure nothing like that ever happened to me again. As unpleasant as the experience was, I alone was responsible for it.

Paradoxically, there was an upside to this painful episode. Without a car, I would take an Uber or a taxi every day to go to Coco Lamela's, five minutes from me. We would share a *maté* then leave for training together. He became a friend and I was happy to reconnect with the ritual I'd shared with Licha in Lyon: *maté* and carpool to practice. At the time, I lived 45 minutes from Tottenham's training centre in Enfield.

My driving ban was reduced to 15 months, following a drink-drive rehabilitation course. Not only did I regain five month's driving, but the experience was positive in itself. There were a dozen of us and it took place in Islington on three successive Mondays in August 2019. Each of us recounted what had happened to us, and then we revised

The Highway Code. The other attendees recognized me on the first Monday, but kept a respectful English distance. The following Monday they started chatting to me about the weekend's football results as soon as I walked in the door. Most were foreigners, like me. There was a Colombian who was setting up his coffee import/export business. Every story was different: a stroke of bad luck, a twist of fate; maybe they'd tried to help someone and it had backfired – like the guy who'd taken the wheel to park the car because his mate wasn't in a fit state.

I liked these sessions. I found myself in the middle of other people's lives, and it was often touching. The instructor was pursued by the papers, I think, but he was an upright chap and didn't tell them a thing. At the second session, he did, however, warn everyone (making as if he wasn't referring to me) that: 'We sometimes get celebrities in here, but what happens here stays in here.' He was a character, and I said to myself that he must have heard some stories in his time. As unwelcome as my misadventure had been, I relished the opportunity to get to know this bunch of people a little.

XIX

The Special One

At least when Tottenham got rid of Mauricio Pochettino in the autumn of 2019, the club didn't replace him with just anyone. Once I'd got over the disappointment, I was happy to get to know José Mourinho. There's a human side to him; he's very close to his players. He's the only manager I've ever seen enter the players' dressing room during practice and sit down for a chat. Even when I had another elbow injury, he came and talked to me once a week. He always had football stories to share; he was a complete enthusiast and an unbelievable bible. Above all, he was someone you felt like following because you said to yourself, 'He'll lead us to victory.' The way a team plays is not essential to him, but he manages to communicate something inspirational.

What might be surprising, though, was the club's choice of a style of play that was the complete opposite of everything we'd been building for five years; a new style of play based on counterattack, whereas with Mauricio we usually held around 60 per cent possession. You might wonder about the logic, even though the justification was a simple one: José is a manager who wins trophies. What with my injured elbow, I had to wait until January 2020 to play for him, against Norwich one Wednesday evening. I saved a penalty against Manchester City, but then, after three Premier League victories in a row, we were outclassed by RB Leipzig, who beat us 0–1 then 3–0 over two legs in the Champions League. We had too many injured players, including Son and Kane, and Leipzig moved too fast. Before the second-leg match on 10 March we started to get a bad feeling: Covid was at our door – Italy was already in the thick of it – and we all felt that life such as we knew it was on borrowed time. Leipzig would be our last match for three months and our last match in front of a crowd until December 2020.

One week later, on 17 March, we learned that Euro 2020 was postponed to 2021. After three months off with an injury, I had only been able to start playing again two months before lockdown. And now the world had stopped. I stayed in London, along with Marine and the children, the club having forbidden the players from leaving the country. But we knew that the Premier League couldn't stay halted for very long, and we started up again quite quickly – in

June, in fact. It was a period where we all refocused on family life, our nearest and dearest, but with a little anxiety too, because Marine and I felt far from Nice and our own family and friends. We'd spent Christmas in London with my grandma and my dad, and Grandma was sick throughout January. We're convinced now that it was Covid she'd had, even then. In Britain restrictions were lifted a little faster than in France: we gradually got the right to go for walks, and it was a period when the weather was very sunny and very warm. For a week we did nothing at all with the club, but then José put in place some training sessions over Zoom. The fitness coaches visited each player's home to deliver equipment. Every morning at 10 a.m. a fitness session at home over Zoom was overseen by José and the staff, who were based at the club. We did cardio training and gym, and they even gave us GPS units so we could go out running every day. It was almost pleasant, under the circumstances, and when lockdown was lifted I was well-honed. Refocusing on our family, our marriage and our three children also did us good. We spent quality time together, and I cooked.

But it was a blessing to be able to play again, even in an empty stadium, despite all the business of vaccines and the endless tests. To respect social distancing, we moved out of our usual dressing room at Tottenham Hotspur Stadium and into the much larger ones on the other side built for the NFL players. We felt that our responsibility to entertain was even stronger than usual. It was more than a role, it was a duty. We were also strongly aware of the club's important community role, primarily through the exceptional outreach work of the Tottenham Hotspur Foundation in the neighbourhood around the stadium – particularly with regard to the elderly and the disadvantaged.

We finished this odd season in sixth place on 26 July 2020, two months later than usual, before starting again on 13 September, free of Amazon and with Gareth Bale back for a year. He didn't have the same dynamite legs, but what ball control, what scoring nous, what sense of positioning! José Mourinho didn't last the full 2020–21 season. Despite topping the league for several weeks in December, an unfortunate series of five defeats in six days in January and February 2021, as well as the unbearable elimination in Zagreb (a 2–0 win but then a 3–0 defeat) in the Europa League in March created tensions around José, who would be fired four days before the final of the League Cup against Manchester City in April. We'd drawn 2–2 against Everton the previous Friday evening, and we had an odd feeling when we arrived at the club on the Monday. Even though I'd got my licence back, Coco Lamela and I still travelled to the club together, sometimes with Giovani Lo Celso. Walking down the corridor to the canteen to get breakfast, we met José on his way to the chairman's office. Shortly afterwards, I was summoned, along with Harry Kane, Eric Dier and Pierre-Emile Højbjerg to a meeting with Daniel Levy, Ryan Mason and Steve Hitchen – then chief scout, later technical director – in an office at the academy. That's where the chairman told us of the club's decision to fire José. It's true that there had been tensions, and José was frustrated with the results and the expectations that he had placed on certain players in a large squad with big egos who weren't so easy to manage. But it was rather surprising to have hired José to win trophies and then sideline him four days before the final which gave him the opportunity of doing just that – an occasion that would have set him against his long-time rival, Pep Guardiola. I had expressed huge public anger after our elimination in Zagreb, declaring that it was a disgrace, but I still found the timing of José's own 'elimination' quite unbelievable. If I'm honest, he didn't have the entirety of the squad behind him, and there were conflicts in the dressing room, but it was still most surprising that a club which had long been reproached for not winning any silverware should take this risk at the very moment when it was in a position to do so, with a manager who knew *how* to do so.

THE SPECIAL ONE

What's true, too, is that there was one José in the first season and another in the second. When we started to lose, he returned to his conflictual approach by shooting at anything that moved. But he held players who worked hard in high esteem, considering them to be true professionals. He would tend to have a go at those who didn't do all they could, in his view, and he was honest; he said what he thought.

At least we were able to say goodbye to him right after training, and then again in the car park later, where we shared a long hug. Four days after that, without José, and with Ryan Mason in the dugout as interim coach, we lost another final, to Manchester City, again without scoring a goal, in a Wembley reduced to just 7,500 spectators, giving away a corner at the end of the match resulting in a goal from Aymeric Laporte. I left Wembley by taxi (I lived a quarter of an hour away) and when the driver dropped me off, I had a bit of a walk instead of going straight home. It was my way of leaving some of this defeat outside the house. Of José's time with us, there also remains the scenes filmed for the Amazon series. I don't think he was playing a role in them. He only watches football, never switches off. Sometimes you don't hear him and sometimes you hear him a lot. He often liked to hang around our goalie training sessions because he had a fondness for us keepers, in memory of his father, perhaps. One day he told me, 'You're part of the last generation of technical keepers.' That stayed with me because the position is evolving towards something else, towards goalies who'll never try to hang onto a ball, but use the whole of their body's surface area instead to deflect it.

As that lugubrious season drew to a close, I was counting on Euro 2021 to bring us a little joy, lightness and victories, particularly with the final being so close to home, at Wembley. Things didn't quite pan out that way. I made an approximate, if simple calculation: 145 caps + 20 matches as substitute + four days' training camp per international match = around 650 days of my life spent with the French national team, which is close to two full years. Sometimes these days seemed very short to me. Other times, they dragged by. So it went for Euro 2021, which didn't leave me with very meaningful memories, even if I would really have liked it to have lasted a little longer.

I didn't appreciate our elimination in the round of 16 against Switzerland (a 3–3 draw followed by defeat on penalties, 4–5) when we were leading 3–1 ten minutes from the end of ordinary time; and I didn't appreciate the context of the final stage split between several countries, against a backdrop of gloomy post-Covid recovery, which prevented us seeing our families throughout the competition.

THE SPECIAL ONE

With the exception of the very particular case of the 2010 World Cup – our luxury hotel in Knysna cut off from the world – I always enjoyed life with the French team in tournaments and have only good memories. But when we found ourselves in downtown Budapest without being able to go out, no chance of stretching our legs or catching a breath of fresh air, it weighed heavily on us. In short, these Euros began with a nice surprise and ended with a very bad one.

The good surprise was Karim Benzema's recall to the squad by Didier Deschamps, after a five-and-a-half-year absence. I've always appreciated Karim, with whom I played at Lyon, and I was happy to see him again and to have confirmation of the superlative professional he had become – meticulous down to the composition of his buffet plate. What still annoys me, even today, is having to remind people of the obvious: I wasn't informed of his return to the squad and never for one moment did I think that the coach should have discussed it with me. I've always known my place; I am merely the team captain. It's a fantasy that I would have had my say regarding the selection.

These Euros should have finished better. We started rather well, with our 1–0 victory over Germany in Munich, and despite our two draws in Budapest against Hungary (1–1) in sweltering heat, then against Portugal (2–2), we finished top of our group. We lost a lot of energy along the way, it's true, as well as our left-backs, since Lucas Hernández and Lucas Digne both picked up injuries. Everything counted in our round of 16 against Switzerland in Bucharest, and everything seemed in place, too, for us to overcome our fatigue, while these absences obliged the coach to rejig our line-up. At a critical moment of the match which could have shaken us, I saved a Ricardo Rodriguez penalty, and we were leading with ten minutes left in ordinary time. The coach's decision to switch to five at the back, with Adrien Rabiot in the left corridor, caused much commentary, but we were leading 3–1 and controlling the match. It was all in our hands but we let it slip away; when you lead 3–1, the score should remain 3–1. We were attracted by the idea of continuing to play, but that's not how we became world champions three years earlier. After going 4–2 ahead against Argentina, we shut up shop and changed our attitude.

Against Switzerland we should have handled things differently and maintained the same level of intensity and effort, instead of alternating phases of balance and imbalance, and not being in agreement, perhaps, about how to manage the last ten minutes. But the images that people debated later – Kingsley Coman's apparent refusal to leave the pitch; the discussion between the coach and Paul Pogba (who seemed to want to continue attacking) – were all over-interpreted and analyzed in light of our elimination, whereas we had always argued on the pitch, it's what had always helped us progress. But Switzerland managed to equalize, sending the match into extra time, and then the penalties arrived. I know how some have summarized this shootout: France were knocked out because Kylian Mbappé flunked his penalty; Hugo Lloris didn't stop a single one; and Didier Deschamps thinks that penalty shootouts are a lottery whereas Switzerland took a more scientific approach.

We were knocked out, first and foremost, because we failed as a squad to avoid a penalty shootout. I'd already been attacked over penalties *before* the match, but I'd saved the one that mattered *during* the match, and that was also a reason for us leading 3–1. It's true that throughout my career I've not had a huge success in this area, even if I've saved some very important penalties, notably during the 2018–19 season with Tottenham. The morning of the round of 16, I'd requested, as usual, the list of Swiss penalty-takers and their preferences – directions, tactics, and so on. That evening I smacked Rodriguez's attempt away in ordinary time, but when it came to the penalty shootout, the Swiss all fired the other way to how they usually did. Penalty shootouts, as we will unfortunately return to later, are always a wrestle between statistics and intuition, and it's not always the statistics which win. It's dodgy to celebrate a 'scientific' approach without knowing what that comprises exactly: the Swiss lost their following penalty shootout in their quarter-final against Spain 1–3 using exactly the same approach as against us. What does 'scientific' even mean? Knowing that so-and-so kicked three of his last four penalties to the right? Everyone has this data. When the coach said that it was a 'lottery', the more simple-minded concluded that he was placing himself in the hands of fate and that he'd done no preparation. That's rubbish. In my view, he only wanted to remind people that since all teams have the same information as their opponents, and since you can never know in advance which players will change direction, you need a little luck too.

The disappointment sat heavily, and the months that followed with Spurs did little to lift it. From Champions League to Europa League to UEFA Conference League, our downgrading was all too clear, and our lack of consistency under José Mourinho highlighted a wider problem: an imbalance in the construction of the squad.

After our seventh place in May 2021, the manager the club found wasn't necessarily its desired one. Nuno Espírito Santo arrived from Wolverhampton, but would only stay

THE SPECIAL ONE

until 1 November 2021. He was named Manager of the Month in August after three victories, but the club vacillated following Harry Kane's request to transfer to Manchester City. Harry had been unjustly targeted for bunking off the start of the new season, even though he had an agreement with Daniel Levy – and I can understand his desire to join Guardiola's City, given how Tottenham seemed to be sliding downhill and it wasn't clear which direction the club wanted to take.

Come September, everything got out of kilter. Nuno didn't want to share the pressure and the leadership, he wanted to bear it all on his own and didn't do himself any favours. Us stalwarts had difficulty finding our place. There wasn't really a connection with him, which resulted in quite a lot of misunderstandings. He seemed to become resigned to things quite quickly, and when things got tough, he didn't try to get close to us veterans. Players need to have confidence in a manager. I belong to a club – that goes without saying – and must give everything to it. But I need to feel that I *want* to give a manager a little more because they inspire me, because they're a guide. Anyone can step onto a pitch with a desire to play, but we need ideas, we need to believe in our manager, and for them to show us that they believe in us.

We were not surprised when Nuno left after our 3–0

defeat to Manchester United. The day after his dismissal, when rumours were flying but no one had told us anything, we saw Antonio Conte arrive at the club. He shook everyone's hand and immediately got to work. Whereas Nuno had perhaps betrayed his own principles by retaining our classic 4-2-3-1 line-up, Conte obviously switched directly to a three at the back and we started by winning nine successive matches in the Premier League. I found him to be quite a character, driven by victory, which gave him energy, but he found it very hard to control his frustration when we started drawing, let alone losing, because his inner torment had to get out; and if he was tormented, then everyone had to share that torment too, and things could get very complicated very fast. He told me once that in any given week, his happiness lasted an hour, just after winning, and that was it. In training, he oversaw everything, organizing tactical sessions with ten outfield players against one goalie; but it was hard for the creative players to find their places in his restrictive game-play. The rigidity of the structure and set sequences did us a lot of good at first but, after a few months, teams learned how to play against us and it became tougher to win.

During matches, Antonio Conte was as extreme and eruptive as he appeared, garnering respect and fear. Such a strong personality pushed wingers to prefer to play on the side opposite the dugout. I have never forgotten our first defeat under Conte: a 2–1 loss to NŠ Mura in Slovenia in the UEFA Conference League. Even though I wasn't playing, I was still entitled to his screams and reproaches, just like everyone else. In squad meetings, we would spend at least 30 minutes a day doing video analysis, not forgetting the interminable preparation camps at our training centre. After the defeat in Maribor, he had screamed: 'Mura, Mura, who's Mura?! We lost to Mura!' I can still hear him.

If a player needed a little love, he'd better not knock at Conte's door. For Conte, trust is earned in training. He has no filter; he's sincere, honest. He's a manager who lives only by results, whereas from a player's perspective, performance is important too. That season, when we lost 3–2 to Manchester United (a Ronaldo hat-trick), a result which didn't reflect our performance, I told Pierre-Emile Højbjerg and Harry Kane in the dressing room: 'They may have just beaten us, but I bet you we finish above them.' And so we did, ending up in fourth place after battering Arsenal 3–0 on the last day, situating ourselves halfway between Conte's demanding nature and a little self-management because, by dint of being whipped and screamed at, we eventually stuck our fingers in our ears.

But at least Conte had a proper direction which he followed. It wasn't easy on a daily basis because he sought perfection; a draw could never satisfy him, even if we played well. With him, there was never any moment less intense than another. As soon as we weren't winning, we knew we had a difficult week ahead. Yet I would tell the youngsters that I would have liked to have had a manager like that at the start of my career, because there is much to be taken on board from such highly demanding standards. Conte turned each defeat into a profound crisis, and had that knack of spreading angst during match preparation, so that we never turned up relaxed. An experienced player knew what to take and what to leave, but a youngster who listened to him attentively for 40 minutes following a training session would be quite dejected. It wasn't easy to freshen up your mindset under such a regime. But he was successful, we recruited some talent (Rodrigo Bentancur, Dejan Kulusevski, Richarlison), and he had my contract extended until autumn 2021. I'll be honest, I don't think the club wanted to extend my contract. Otherwise, Conte would have come to see me over the summer, and Fabio Paratici, our director of football, wouldn't have taken on loan an Italian goalie, Pierluigi Gollini – very popular in the dressing room, a super guy, very respectful and a bit wacky. When I spoke to Paratici that summer, he dodged the question over extending my contract: 'We'll see in six months.' But in six months I'd have been out of contract.

When Conte arrived, everything changed. He was very clear with me: 'There are rumours that I want this or that goalie. It's not true. What do you want to do?' I replied that I had no issues with his demanding standards and that I was with him all the way. And so in January 2022 I demanded a two-year extension, with the appropriate remuneration, so as not to have to wonder what I was going to do six months out from a World Cup. The club said yes, but I had the distinct impression that the confidence came more from the manager than from the bosses.

Many and exceptional were the circumstances which explained the end of the relationship between Conte and Spurs. He wasn't the same over the following season after the sudden death of our athletic trainer, Gian Piero Ventrone, in October 2022 from acute leukaemia. Ventrone and Conte were close friends and long-time collaborators, and Gian Piero was the only one who could reason with Antonio, and to whom the coach would turn when he had second thoughts. On the eve of the World Cup, we lay in fourth place, and were still there in mid-March. But the team had run out of steam and the coach would lose his patience over the slightest thing. It made sense, really: Conte was living in a hotel, without his wife or daughter, and his friend had died. All of which conspired to make his life somewhat unbalanced, and led to him becoming even more obsessive. Then he got sick and had to have surgery on his gallbladder, but came back to work too soon and was then obliged to return home because of the pain. On 6 January another death hit him, that of his friend Gianluca Vialli. Conte turned into someone I no longer recognized, and understandably so. When he returned to London in March, he made a number of critical statements about the club, and when he went back to Italy during the international break, the club asked him to stay there. His staff were still in London and ran training sessions, but his assistant Cristian Stellini would soon be replaced by Ryan Mason, to wrap up a season worth forgetting. I had one year left on my contract. I knew it was over, that I would never play for Tottenham again. I couldn't have known, though, that the goodbyes would take so long.

XX

Au Revoir Les Bleus!

When I played the 2022 World Cup I made the most of each day with Les Bleus, never wondering if it would be my last. I sensed that the void would come pretty quick, and I only hoped that it would wait until the day of the final, on the afternoon of Sunday 18 December in Doha. What I retain of that day is a dream, a torment and a void combined, with just a few centimetres between them, at the end of a long World Cup final, the like of which has never been seen before. I began this book with a description of the moments just after the final whistle and the regrets I had: I know full well that I carry them still and that they will leave me slowly, if they ever do.

Our 2022 World Cup, which finished so badly, didn't start that well either: too many injuries, too many controversies and insufficient preparation (just two days at Clairefontaine). I said to myself: 'This is surely your last World Cup,

AU REVOIR LES BLEUS!

Hugo, make the most of it!' But I was thinking about so many other things too, what with all the human rights issues surrounding Qatar – women's rights; LGBT+ rights – not to mention environmental concerns; they weighed us down. I know that the captain of the French national team has an important voice. We are people, too; we don't just care about footie. We all have a conscience and values to defend. But it's also because I was captain that I had to make a distinction between my personal values and our collective ones. For the press conferences, I didn't want to prepare any stock phrases which would have better protected me when asked certain questions; I didn't want to trot out any mechanical replies. Well, too bad if I got shot down in France for my poorly prepared answers and for trying to explain that it wasn't up to me to preach. Do we handle these issues so much better in France that we can dole out lessons as we travel the world? I could have gone further, perhaps, amplified my message, my defence of certain values, but I remained cautious because I was representing the whole squad, not just myself. I couldn't wear the rainbow armband because FIFA didn't let us: no captain was allowed to wear it. Even though my sensibility veered towards most of the struggles that were so noisily promoted on the occasion of this World Cup in Qatar, I found their manipulation and the surrounding hypocrisy tiresome. Things were expected of footballers which weren't expected of others. When French museums opened branches in Arab countries, I don't recall the French dignitaries wearing rainbow armbands.

Meanwhile the squad was nursing an epidemic of injuries. We had already lost Paul Pogba and N'Golo Kanté. When Christopher Nkunku hurt his knee one evening at Clairefontaine, it was immediately obvious from his scream of pain that he'd be laid up for a while. With Karim Benzema, we didn't see it coming because not only had he been taking it relatively easy, he'd received the Ballon d'Or three weeks earlier and this was supposed to be *his* World Cup. He was slowly returning to training after a little muscular issue, and was not far off a full return to the squad, training separately with Raph Varane, until the day he joined a small group drill, which he left almost immediately. When I asked after him following our evening meal, they told me he'd gone off for some scans. I learned of his withdrawal at one in the morning, from a friend's text, then by checking the internet. I was shocked, but I said to myself that I'd see him the next morning. But when I got up, he had already left. It was weird to not even be able to say goodbye. But I didn't resent him for it; I've known Karim for a long time and I know how modest he is. Everyone reacts in their own way, and nobody wants to show their hurt. I would simply have liked to bid him farewell. I don't believe that story of how some players were happy to see him go. We were about to embark on a major competition three days later, and we couldn't allow ourselves to be weighed down, or to think that we were cursed. Otherwise we'd have thrown in the sponge from the first few minutes of the first match against Australia after the injury which would put Lucas Hernández out of the competition. Instead, we won 4–1. We're programmed to adapt, not to lament, to rely upon experienced players who've been in such big competitions before, to regroup from tricky situations, to create new dynamics and progress, match after match. We never said or thought that it was better without Karim and the other injured players. But it was important that we believed deep down that we just had to get on with it and that we could still make it through to the end. Antoine Griezmann, for example, would reinvent himself as a midfielder in the coach's new 4-3-3 system. He had the time of his life, totally liberated. Olivier Giroud gave his all and Kylian remained this extraordinary player who would tip the balance in every match and for nearly every goal. And there were youngsters playing in their first World Cup, guys like Adrien Rabiot, Aurélien Tchouaméni, Théo Hernandez and Dayot Upamecano, who would pull off some amazing feats.

The second match, against Denmark, who had beaten us twice in the previous six months, was our test, in that funny stadium built from 974 shipping containers. We won 2–1 and went through to the round of 16, in a match watched by Marine and the girls, my father, his partner, Ester, and my grandma. They'd bought one-way tickets, no returns booked, which was pretty far-sighted of them. Neither Australia nor Denmark caused us any bother and, having talked about it with them, I know that the Danes were troubled by the controversy over their muted kit designs – and the black third kit honouring migrant workers who had died in the construction industry in Qatar – but a World Cup demands so much energy, you can't waste it on anything else.

We progressed through the competition step by step, so our 1–0 defeat to Tunisia, in a magnificent atmosphere, following Antoine Griezmann's famous disallowed goal, was of little consequence. We'd got used to losing our third group matches, the only ones where the result itself doesn't always matter, but everything else does because it's an opportunity to play, to stay alert, to continue to push the first choice players, ready to replace them when the moment comes, as we saw in the final. I was happy, on behalf of the squad, for Steve Mandanda to play another World Cup match, owing to our long shared history. Back in 2018 I'd responded very positively to the idea, particularly since Steve had missed out on the 2014 World Cup because of injury. The principle is that the number 1 goalie has priority according to requirements, but since a keeper doesn't just come on for 20 minutes, as an outfield player would, it's above all a question of how long and how beneficial a break for the number 1 goalie should be. It was a discussion I had with the goalie trainer, Franck Raviot, never with Steve. He and I didn't need to. In 2022, the only new factor in the equation was the imminence of the caps record, but I maintained exactly the same line and the same principle as that which had worked in 2018. Playing for only the caps record would not have been a good reason, even if not doing so imperilled it. And I was convinced that I'd break the record anyway. I noted that other World Cup winning goalies had not given their stand-ins any match-time, which I found odd. Franck always made sure that his little group of goalkeepers had the right mindset and that we all looked out for each other; throughout my career, we all got along very well.

During the World Cup, I really loved my regular meet-ups with the children of the Lenval Foundation (attached to Nice's Lenval Children's Hospital), of which I am the patron. To let them experience the World Cup from the inside, I had committed to keeping a logbook for which I would write a new entry once a week, as well as filming a half-hour video answering the children's questions after each match. The montage was broadcast on the hospital's TV screens and it became a big hit. When I was younger, this might have taken up too much energy and concentration, but at nearly 36 years old I was familiar enough with myself to know that I could do it well, and I think that it was a good thing to do. I really liked their questions and I hope they liked my answers.

Our round of 16 match against Poland would be my 142nd cap, pulling me level with the record holder, Lilian Thuram. I didn't even think about whether it would be my last cap; I didn't want to add that personal element to the already enormous pressure of a World Cup knockout match. We handled this rendezvous quite well because with a round of 16 comes a whole other logic, a whole other ambition and all sorts of feelings. Olivier Giroud scored just before half-time off an assist from Kylian, who wrapped things up with two goals – while I conceded a Robert Lewandowski penalty right at the end of the match, after stopping his first attempt. I moved a touch too soon and I knew, as I saved it, that it would have to be taken again. I had already punched away a penalty for nothing against Leicester that season because my heel was slightly above the line.

When we beat Poland 3–1 and I equalled the caps record,

AU REVOIR LES BLEUS!

I already knew that I would break it one day. It was a very powerful feeling, particularly as, in all those years, I had never sought to nab an extra cap here or there, and I'd let Steve play the third group game because it was the right thing to do – all of which made it an even more beautiful way of beating Lilian Thuram's record 16 years after he'd set it. In the run-up to the World Cup in Qatar, I had always refused to talk about the record or give interviews in advance to be broadcast during the tournament; I even said no to a documentary about the 142 caps. This was partly superstition, maybe, but also respect for the World Cup and the dramas that come with it.

Lilian Thuram had picked up 142 caps; I stopped at 145. I know that one day I will hand one of my former teammates a shirt bearing the number 146 – I just don't know who yet. Logically, it will be either Antoine Griezmann or Kylian Mbappé. I'll try to enjoy my record while it lasts, but outfield players' careers are lasting longer and longer, and us goalies never come on just for a few minutes. If I had come on for ten minutes each time I was Steve's sub, I would no doubt have over 160 caps. Kylian will do it comfortably, that's for sure, and the only question is whether Antoine will do it first.

England added to the majestic, electric framing of the World Cup quarter-final. I feared the English: I knew them all and I sensed that something was happening with them following their World Cup semi-final in 2018 and their Euro final in 2021. Plus my mate Harry Kane was playing for them. After Aurélien Tchouaméni's goal in the first half, it was Harry who equalized from an avoidable penalty. And after Olivier Giroud confirmed what an exceptional scorer he still was, at 36, it was again Harry who took to the penalty spot opposite me, in the 84th minute, at a moment when things were looking shaky and we risked losing.

Thinking about penalties before the match, someone had said to me, 'It's a good thing you know him well.' But it was not, in fact, a good thing, because when you really know Harry Kane well, you know how capable he is of changing things up and striking in any part of the goal with the same precision and power from the same run-up. Still, I knew that he had a strong tendency to kick powerful shots across the keeper, particularly in big matches, but what should I do with this information? On his first penalty, I thought he knew that I knew that he would make a powerful strike across the goal, so I dived to my left and was wrong-footed. VAR prolonged the wait before his second penalty, and I recall asking Antoine for his striker's intuition: 'Reckon he'll switch it up, Antoine?'

'No, I don't think so.'

So I dived right. Harry saw this, of course, and as soon

AU REVOIR LES BLEUS!

as the ball left his foot, I knew it was going over the bar. If he had equalized, it would have been another story, because we were at breaking point. England were impressive, both with their shots and how they pressed us.

At the final whistle my first feeling was joy, pure, unadulterated joy; and the second was for Harry. I went to see him and we hugged, but he was inconsolable, and words were of little use. We hadn't exchanged any texts before the match, but I would message him afterwards: 'I'm thinking about you a lot. I have huge respect and admiration for you. Part of me shares the hurt you might be feeling. I wish you the best. Make the most of the break, rest up.' He answered that there were no words that could console him, but he wished me the best for the rest of the competition.

Lilian Thuram was there in the dressing room: we took a selfie together. Léandro had stayed at the hotel, but I broke the caps record in front of my whole family, except for my brother, who would arrive for the final. I was washed out after having beaten England. It took me a few minutes to get myself together and to let the nervous tension fall away after such a hard match and a wearisome pre-match, with that recurring question: 'How do you feel about the fact that the English see you as the weak point of the team?' But I know how journos are and they'd gone after Kylian, too. We answered them on the pitch, where I'd notably won a duel with Harry and punched clear a Jude Bellingham strike. In the dressing room, the coach gave me a special '143' shirt that everyone had signed.

Victory over England was a huge moment, because no one believed in us at the start of the tournament – what with the absences and the notorious curse of the outgoing champion, which we'd had to endure people lecturing us about for the past year. But I'd loved being the reigning champion over the four years preceding the competition, and in Qatar I loved being the outgoing champion, the team to beat, with that golden 'World Champions' badge on our chests. In beating England we showed them all that the champions were still standing, in spite of everything.

Two days before the semi-final against Morocco, the coach called us together and told us, 'Get ready, guys!' We looked at each other: 'What on earth's he talking about?' He played a video showing the atmosphere at Morocco's quarter-final match against Portugal, and added, 'Guys, get ready to not hear anything.' When we got there, we loved the atmosphere in the Al-Bayt stadium for the semi-final, which I thought was wonderful. We were heading towards the final with players we'd not been expecting two years earlier; players such as Youssouf Fofana, a great chap, real team player, always positive, always going all-in whether for five minutes or a whole match, simply happy to be there.

We made things easy by scoring very fast thanks to Théo Hernández; and as we approached the end of the match, Randal Kolo Muani put paid to the suspense. Even though we weren't really scared, you can't qualify for a World Cup final without feeling intense emotion. I have much admiration for how Morocco (my grandma's homeland) plotted their path to the semis, and much respect for the work of their coach Walid Regragui, whom I would include on my list of suggestions for the annual Best FIFA Football Coach Award, which the worldwide federation asks managers and captains to make.

We spent some fine moments together as a squad in the days leading up to the final. Antoine, Olivier, Raph and I had the habit of indulging in a glass of red wine or a light beer after dinner on the evening before a match day, for which the coach would take the mickey out of us: 'Hey, it's the centenarians' club!' Raph was not a centenarian – the final would be his 93rd and final cap – but he liked to hang out with us, so we co-opted him. The four of us had experienced so much together.

I first met Raphaël Varane when he was just 18, and I sensed that he'd be with us for a good while. Poised, calm, intelligent, with an exemplary record, he was always ready to take on responsibilities, and kept his head on his shoulders. The reason I was able to remain captain for so long was because I could rely on leaders such as Raph, Olivier, Antoine, Paul, Blaise and, later, Kylian. I saw how Raph had gradually carved out a sizeable place for himself in the team. In my leadership, I've always left a lot of room for others. When you look at Raph's career, his achievements and how he's managed to deal with his knee issues, it's exceptional – not forgetting the courage, at 29 years old, to take the decision to leave the French national team. He's an awesome fellow.

Olivier has had an unusual career. Success came relatively late, and his ability to always bounce back and to keep going is an example of mental fortitude. Every time you think he's done, he returns: he's there, he scores, he breaks records. His statistics speak for themselves. What unites us all is our love of the blue shirt, and all of the incredible things we have experienced together. I know these men as players, as fathers, as husbands. They're great guys. There's a part of me which, as a sports lover, admires everything they've accomplished. And they're guys with true values, who've got their feet on the ground, who are not cut off from life but plugged into contemporary society.

In Qatar the youngest players' respect for me was clear: I felt it when we knocked out England and I broke the record. They were happy for me, they told me so, and showed it. They were kids when I started, but I've always held them in high regard. I've spent more time with some than others, it's true, but I've talked to them all.

I've measured the passage of time, too, by noticing Kylian's impact on my own children. During the World Cup we took a photo with Kylian and the girls at our training base, and Anna-Rose was almost stressed because it was Kylian, even though we've played together for a long time and I was his captain. But I can really understand what he represents for them, and it touched me too. I've watched Kylian's evolution. We had a chat together in February 2022, around the time he was fighting for his image rights after threatening to boycott the sponsors' photoshoot. Before a meeting with Noël Le Graët, the president of the French Football Federation, I went to see Kylian in his room to tell him that we were behind him, that what was an individual issue needed to become a collective one and that we would settle it together. Which we did. The thing that his people didn't like about the image contract was what we had all thought for many years: it wasn't suited to the new generation and the way football was going, let alone the space occupied by Kylian, and I could understand that he didn't always want to be first in line for all the sponsors.

Group dynamics in the final stages of a competition have always been essential to performance, not to mention enjoyment which, as much as the achievements, is what we remember. It's always a united squad that progresses to the final. In Qatar I remember that we tried to console Benjamin Pavard after he was sidelined from the team – or perhaps sidelined himself, I don't know exactly what happened, just that it was our role to support him, to keep him with us.

In Qatar we didn't have anything approaching the Istra fire extinguisher incident. Everything was much calmer, with discussions beside the pool and barbecues on the terrace. Everyone could have their own little rituals without bothering anyone else. In the morning, I would come down to breakfast, then head to the gym, take a cold bath to recover, and later a short swim before lunch, followed by a siesta under the air conditioning, lulled by the call to prayer. I didn't feel the need to go out, particularly since the coach had made sure to include some family time in our schedule. There was no tension, because life was beautiful, we were winning, and also because the squad had been composed with a view to making it all go smoothly.

But in the days and hours leading up to our second World Cup final in a row, a shiver of concern rushed through our ranks, and a touch of fever too. There was a virus going around. At such a moment in history, the consequences could be so huge that it was hard to escape the paranoia. Obviously, we all wondered where this virus came from. There hadn't been any such issues thus far, there hadn't

AU REVOIR LES BLEUS!

been any elsewhere – yet there was a virus in our camp. Adrien Rabiot would stay in his room for a good while, Raph wasn't in great shape, and several players were totally depleted. We had the impression of not being able to fight with all our resources, and being under-resourced compared to other teams.

Our other feeling upon arriving at the stadium on the day of the final was that it was filled with Argentinians; that it was as if everyone else wanted Leo Messi to win because that would have been the best narrative as far as FIFA and Qatar were concerned. This meant we'd not only be playing against Argentina, but against the whole world. In order for this World Cup to go down in history, Messi had to finally become a world champion. Meanwhile, we were fighting a virus which had infected only us.

But the reality was that we started out not really playing this final. We were somewhere else. They knocked us sideways, although I should say that the refereeing appeared to be more favourable to the Argentinians, given how many calls went against us. From the start, Cristian Romero had it in for me. He really hurt me, and it was clearly on purpose, yet Szymon Marciniak, the Polish referee, who strongly denied any bias against France in the game, said nothing. Cuti is a mate, we played together at Tottenham and he lived in the house next door. I was crazy angry when it happened, and I swore at him, because he didn't even come over to apologize. But I couldn't really reproach him for being that way, because he was also like that when we played in the same team. When you see what he's capable of in training, you have no doubt what he'll do in a match. It's how he plays and how he tries to win with his team. The problem is that he didn't receive the card he deserved, which would have checked him. He came up to me at the end of the match, embarrassed, sincere, but I straight away told him: 'Enjoy this moment, we'll talk later.' That he came to talk to me in such a euphoric moment, as a world champion, to say, '*Hermano*, I'm sorry,' shows that he's not a bad guy. Blokes like him are often big softies off the pitch, but in training Cuti would be capable of tackling his own son.

I'm convinced, too, that the first penalty was barely justified and that if the ref hadn't blown his whistle VAR wouldn't have halted play to give it. But the coach sensed that we were all at sea, completely destabilized, and so at 2–0 down, just before the interval, he decided not to wait to substitute Olivier Giroud and Ousmane Dembélé with Marcus Thuram and Randal Kolo Muani. At half-time I was dazed. Olivier was also down at heart, but he managed to rally us all, saying that it wasn't over. Steve piped up too, Kylian also, and when we stepped back on the pitch we were determined to change the way it was going. As it happened, we managed to change nothing at all for a good half hour. I don't know if the Argentinians eased off because they couldn't maintain the same pressure, or whether our youngsters had better legs, but when Kylian scored his penalty they began to ask themselves questions they'd not asked in a long while. Up until that point there was no reason to think that we could become world champions in their stead, and nothing we could do allowed us to hope that. But between the penalty and Kylian's second goal, from 2–0 down to 2–2, from inevitable defeat to the craziest hope, we experienced the wildest 90 seconds in the history of the World Cup. At 2–2 this final became something else: a boxing match on a tightrope stretched 50 metres above the void.

At the toss before extra time to decide the ends and who would kick off, the referee told me: 'They thought it was all over.' I'd have preferred it had he told me nothing and not stopped play, for example, to give us a free-kick even though Kingsley Coman was in full counterattack. Argentina seized back the advantage (3–2) just after we changed ends: I'd managed to push away the ball at point-blank range, but, of course, it had to end up at Leo's feet. Still, we told ourselves that we hadn't pulled ourselves back to 2–2 to just give up now, and even though the ref had had it in for us a bit at times, he did award us two penalties.

Kylian converted the second one and Emiliano Martínez deprived us of a third star on our national strip by saving from Randal Kolo Muani in the final minute of extra time. As always, it came down to a few centimetres.

Just before the penalty shootout I spent a few minutes alone on the bench. Franck Raviot came over and we chatted a little, but then I needed to be alone. It was good to sit for a bit because I was quite physically wiped out. I took a towel, a little water and some energy liquid and started to think, to get into my bubble. I lost the toss and so the shootout would take place at the Argentinian end, but I chose France to shoot first.

The prospects didn't look very good for us: Argentina had already won their quarter-final against the Netherlands on penalties, and two penalty specialists, Lautaro Martínez and Paulo Dybala, had just come on with this in mind. With the exception of Kylian, we no longer had a single penalty-taker on the pitch. Most of the guys who'd shortly be doing the honours had never taken a penalty for their club. Our usual penalty-takers were either absent or had come off during the final – as was the case for Olivier Giroud, Ousmane Dembélé and Antoine Griezmann.

Kylian scored and I found myself facing Leo Messi. Recently he had started changing his run-up and placing his shot according to the goalie's movements. During his

AU REVOIR LES BLEUS!

run-up I therefore took a small step to shift position in order to be able to dive to my right at the very last moment: I was a few centimetres short. Then Kingsley Coman missed his and Dybala stepped forward. I knew that his preference was for a powerful shot across goal. But Martínez would explain later that after saving Kingsley's penalty, he'd advised Dybala to shoot down the middle: 'When I make a save in a shootout, the pressure is on the other goalie, so he'll dive. More than anything, in a World Cup final you don't want to look stupid by simply standing there in the middle.' So Dybala shot down the middle, and, honestly, it didn't miss my foot by very much. Sometimes I can still feel it. Next, Aurélien Tchouaméni stepped up and Martínez went much too far. I said what I thought about this at the start of the book, and how strongly FIFA had ruled against Szymon Marciniak by changing its regulations so that a referee can stop a goalie trying to destabilize a penalty-taker like that. When Aurélien missed, I realized I would have to stop two to equalize, three to win. I touched the ball on Paredes' shot, and my very slightly delayed reaction time was because I wondered if he might put it down the middle, too. Next, Kolo, who gave a textbook demo of how to do just that: his shot smashed straight down the middle. Finally, Gonzalo Montiel, on whom there was no pressure because Argentina were two penalties up at that point. I'd seen on videos how he liked to take it straight-on after a long run-up. And this time he swept it across me. Argentina were world champions.

After that, it was like a shutter came down. I was shattered, unaware of anything, alone amid the euphoria of the Argentinians. We had to remain on the pitch for a much longer ceremony than expected, watching it all, enduring it all. I was painfully aware of the centimetres by which we'd lost, and my responsibility as goalie. There is no grey zone in penalty shootouts. As a goalie, you're either a hero or you're nothing. I had a heavy responsibility during that World Cup because not only was I the goalie, but I was captain too – not to mention that I'd been in the squad a long time, and longevity excuses nothing. Everything which had multiplied the joy four years earlier in Moscow now multiplied the disappointment in Qatar. As goalie, and captain, I should have been able to do something. After a victory, I never felt more of a winner than my teammates, but after a defeat I always felt a little more of a loser.

Even today, I must still applaud Argentina and try to remember that it's an exceptional thing to qualify for a World Cup final four years after having won it. But we had no opportunity to get over those emotions. Even those who won that final didn't get over it easily. So imagine what it was like for those who lost.

XXI

Life After

The final ten months at Spurs, when I didn't play, gave me time to think about what my life would be like when I stopped being a footballer. And then we signed for Los Angeles FC and I became nothing but a footballer again for one, two or three more years. I was in no hurry to retire as a player and neither am I in any hurry to wonder about what might come next. I might have a better idea when that time comes.

I say 'we' signed because I didn't go to LA alone. There are five of us living in Los Angeles now, in a house in Encino with a garden and a swimming pool to enjoy the sun, which we didn't have in London. Every morning, at nearly the same time, I head off to train at LAFC, in the east of the city, while Marine takes Anna-Rose, Giuliana and Léandro to school. Marine likes to say that 'home is anywhere the five of us are together'. She's so right.

But, at 37, this is no pre-retirement, it's a competitive career continuing differently. LAFC want to win the American title. Me too. I can't not train to the max, not play to the max and not hate defeat. So in Los Angeles I'll continue to live my passion to the full and refuse to lose, in a club whose interpersonal, family aspects I adore. I'll be able to share everything with Marine and the kids. I want us to make happy memories here, together.

I left Tottenham following the sort of goodbye I'd dreamed of. After 12 years and 447 matches for Spurs, Daniel Levy gifted me an exit that I'll never forget. The elegant manner in which he terminated my contract enabled me to choose LAFC without worrying about having the smallest salary in my career since my earliest days at Nice. And, on a personal level, he arranged for me to bid the club and the fans farewell at half-time of a Spurs match on 31st December 2023, following a warm and touching lunch together. All's well that ends well. I know that autumn was very tough for me, but had I left earlier – the previous summer, for example – to go to a European club who would have offered me no guarantee of first-team football, nor an interesting challenge, the stars would not have aligned so well.

We'll be living far from France for a while, and it's possible that I'll feel like going back there more often. I've long thought that if I let go, if I looked back instead of being completely focused on the next match, I would pay the price for it. It seems to me that I can do two things at once from now on: appreciate what I've done, and focus on what I have still to do. With age, I have started easing up on myself. As a younger man, I wouldn't sleep after a defeat: I'd go over the match in my head, analyzing it all. I find it easier now. Even a bad training session could drive me crazy – with myself, or with a teammate; it gnawed at me. But I also know that this dissatisfaction has always been my strength. I was like that from the start because I knew exactly what I wanted. When my grandpa, who had nurtured these high standards, died, the little voice in my head remained. But I realize now that I also owe this temperament – this rigour, this lack of half-measures – to my parents and how I was brought up. As a teenager, if I lost on a Sunday it was going to school the next day that helped me get over it. I could never have gone to a training academy and done nothing but football; I needed high school and my friends to re-centre myself and take my mind off things.

We have all made sacrifices. My parents by working. My sister by going off to study far from home. Me by leaving.

LIFE AFTER

Gautier by staying. I would have liked to have spent more time with them, and supported my brother better after my mother died. There was the geographical distance, and that of our natural reserve: you have to look for signs in our family, rather than waiting for words, which will probably never come.

In those months when I wasn't playing, I was able to go and cheer on Gautier at Le Havre. He was on the pitch and I was in the stands with my dad. I recall back in October 2012 being asked about his first appearance on the teamsheet, for a League Cup match against Olympique Lyonnais, and how I'd answered that he still had his *baccalauréat* to pass.

He turned pro even younger than I did (and he did pass his *baccalauréat*, with merit). I admire my brother for having dealt with so many obstacles. It can't have been easy for him to be 'the brother of . . .' In fact, it says 'G. Lloris' on his shirt. I have never asked him why, but I have an idea, of course. He has had so many injuries, and he was so academically bright, that my dad and I wondered if he shouldn't resolve to seek success elsewhere, in another field. He would have succeeded anywhere. But he never gave up, even though each time he got his head above water, a new injury took him down again, whether at Gazélec Ajaccio, Nice or Auxerre, too, where he got injured on his birthday, in July, while I was on holiday and my dad, Grandma and I had shown up to surprise him. Incredible, really: he discovered we were there during the warm-up – we waved to him from the stands – and during the match he fractured his metatarsal. We spent the rest of his birthday in A&E. I've sometimes wondered what I would have done in his stead, if I would have fought through it all. But I back him all the way. I've always watched his matches, even when I was far away and he was playing in the juniors (I would catch the highlights streamed on the OGC Nice website). It's easier these days because he's on the telly – if I can't watch the game live, I'll catch the highlights.

Since my career has continued, I can look back (without nostalgia), and it's an entirely new feeling for me. I see the players, the clubs, the world championship title, the records, my three nominations for the Ballon d'Or in 2016, 2018 and 2019 – memories that I keep close to my heart, in a corner of my mind and in a few drawers. When I go over to my grandma's, I sometimes take a peek at everything she's kept in my old room where I used to do my homework after school: my shirts, my first cups, my under-19 European Champions medal, a Toulon Tournament best goalie medal, and lots of other things. At home, I don't have anything laid out or on display; I don't need to show off. But one day, I'll surely frame the important shirts, perhaps one from each of my four homes (Nice, Lyon, Tottenham, Les Bleus), because they're a part of me. I'll also leave a space for LAFC. Meanwhile, I accumulate. I've got a trunk full of shirts: the yellow one from the playoff against Ireland; shirts from the goalies who've inspired me (Buffon, Casillas, Barthez, Júlio César); the Real Madrid one that José Mourinho gave me. And I've got another trunk full of pairs of boots and gloves. I give many away, to friends and to charities, but I've kept a few for myself too. By the way, I think it's a pity that you can't easily buy our goalie shirts in fan shops. It's our life: everyone says, 'Allez les Bleus!' – but us goalies never play in blue.

One way, at least, I've prepared for the future is by always being sensible with money. When I was little, Grandma – who would have got excellent grades in arts and crafts during my school years and those of my brother – made me a piggy bank from a tennis ball box, which she'd wrapped in paper to look pretty, before cutting a slit in the lid to put the coins in. I have always saved. Over time, I began to develop an interest in investments and in managing my assets, and my dad was a very good source of advice, of course. I've had my fingers in everything, from financial and property investments, with the help of my lawyers, Pierre and Aude, to start-ups – such as Cédric Messina's

MyCoach personal fitness app – where the human aspect is key as far as I'm concerned.

My expertise lies in football – it's been my life since childhood – but I have no problem with the idea of having to reinvent myself. I'm sure I must have saved time by rubbing shoulders with top-level managers and chairmen. I'll always prefer a good workout on the pitch, but I've enjoyed having to deal with the business side of things, handling everything myself, negotiating my salary or team bonuses with the members of the board. You grow up fast in this business; you learn to be distrustful. As soon as I began earning money from football, I told myself I'd immediately put some away to enjoy myself later. In the end, I didn't have to wait too long. When I see the difficulties that some former players face, I tell myself that you need to be sensible and above all not imagine a lifestyle you can't maintain. At any rate, sport will always be a part of my life, whether it's tennis, padel or skiing.

Of course, I wonder about a future in football. I can't yet know how much I'll still need the adrenaline that I craved when I didn't play for ten months. I can't imagine doing regular punditry – but for a major competition, why not? Whether keeping one foot in the game, returning now and then, getting used to being away from it a bit, or never leaving, I'd like to find the right equilibrium, as I watch

LIFE AFTER

my kids grow up, being there to support and guide them until they reach adult life, even though I've been warned that being a dad never ends.

Manager? I don't know. There are days when I'm tempted by the job, but the idea of living and breathing footie 24 hours a day holds me back a little. I've never underestimated the role of a manager, or the time it takes, the energy and the sacrifices it involves. Those are aspects I would need to take into consideration, and I'm not sure that I'm ready for it. For the moment, I tell myself this crazy life is not for me. But there are other roles in football, other possible destinies: the ideal, in my eyes, would be to have, or to be part of, a club and to mould it, both on and off the pitch. I want to have some responsibility; I don't want to stay in football if it means taking a passive role. Meanwhile, and especially if I'm still in Los Angeles, I'd really like to be a pundit for the 2026 World Cup in the United States, Mexico and Canada. I played in the four previous World Cups, and I'd almost be at home. In any event, we'll go to watch the matches of Les Bleus as a family, like before. I'll no longer be on the pitch, but among my friends and loved ones, and that'll be beautiful too.

The French national team, the World Cup and my family united are among my loveliest memories. I often look at that photo, taken in the minutes following the 2018 final and our world champions title. It's one of my favourites Anna-Rose, Giuliana and the World Cup in my arms. Along with my son Léandro, they are my most precious trophies. I remember the rain, the confetti and the heat of the storm just before it broke. I remember the happiness.

Index

N.B. HL is used as an abbreviation for Hugo Lloris throughout the index.

A
Abardonado, Pancho 63
Abbiati, Christian 71
Abdoun, Djamel 54
Abidal, Éric 107, 110, 115, 131, 153
Adebayor, Manu 186
African Cup of Nations 167
Agüero, Sergio 191, 192
Ajaccio, AC 53
Ajax, AFC 192, 193-4
Albania National Football Team 167
Algeria 34
Amazon documentary, Tottenham Hotspur FC 181, 182, 197-8, 201, 238-9
Anelka, Nicolas 93, 95, 105-8, 110, 114, 119-20, 224
Anigo, José 176
Antonetti, Frédéric 54, 55, 56, 57, 60, 63, 66-7, 130
APOEL FC 127
Areola, Alphonse 221
Argentina National Football Team 1, 3, 10, 209-11, 241, 266-71
arrest for drunk driving, HL's 226-31

Arsenal FC 130, 137, 141, 143, 191, 246
AS sports newspaper 166
Aston Villa FC 140-1
Atlético de Madrid 71
Aubameyang, Pierre-Emerick 191
Aulas, Jean-Michel 75, 86-7, 108, 110, 122-3, 137-8, 139, 167
Aurier, Serge 182
Australia National Football Team 208, 254
Austria National Football Team 93

B
Ba, Ibrahim 224
Bachelot, Roselyne 115
Bah, Abdallah 47
Bale, Gareth 236
Baratelli, Dominique 42, 43, 47
Barcelona, FC 80, 101, 191, 193, 198
Barthez, Fabien 16, 59, 61, 92, 94-5, 177, 278
Bastos, Michel 82, 180
Bataclan terror attack (2015) 161-2
Baticle, Gérald 126
Batistuta, Gabriel 34-5

283

INDEX

Bats, Joël 16, 71-2, 75-6, 77, 97-8, 126, 139, 177
Bayer Leverkusen 214-15
Bayern Munich, FC 80, 86, 198
beach soccer tournaments 53
Belgium National Football Team 217-18
Bellingham, Jude 261
Ben Afra, Hatem 135
Bentancur, Rodrigo 247
Benzema, Karim 76, 80, 83, 153, 156, 158, 160, 163-4, 165-6, 240, 253-4
Bini, Bruno 41-2, 91
Blanc, Laurent 100, 129, 131, 132, 133, 134-5, 147
Bodmer, Mathieu 76
Bordeaux, FC Girondins de 71, 79, 81, 85, 110, 124, 128, 215
Borussia Dortmund 191
Bosnia National Football Team 216
Boulon, Philippe 67
Boumsong, Jean-Alain 76
Braida, Ariedo 71
Brazil National Football Team 217
Brentford FC 6, 9
Brigade Sud ultras 58
Bruneton, Régis 36-7, 42, 178
Bucharest-FCSB 80
Buffon, Gigi 59, 278
Bulgaria National Football Team 153, 206
Buscher, Gérard 39, 53

C

Cabaye, Yohan 48, 52, 54, 153
Cáceres, Martín 213
Cañizares, Santiago 34
Cannes, AS 58
Carnus, Georges 41-2
Casillas, Iker 59, 83, 278
Cavani, Edinson 212
Cedac de Cimiez 20, 36-7, 42, 43, 178
César, Júlio 64, 278
Champions League, UEFA 40, 72, 79, 80, 82-4, 85-7, 99, 126-7, 169, 181, 187-8, 190-7, 206, 215, 234

Châteauroux FC, LB 56
Chelsea FC 140, 188
Cherrad, Malek 55
Cheyrou, Benoît 94
Chiellini, Giorgio 205
China National Football Team 102
Cissokho, Aly 82
Clattenburg, Mark 171
Cohen, Maurice 51, 60, 71, 75, 216
Colchester United FC 198
Collège Raoul Dufy, Nice 40
Collot, Patrick 77
Coman, Kingsley 242, 268, 270
Comolli, Damien 70
concussion protocols 151-2
Conte, Antonio 6-7, 11-12, 16, 22, 23, 31, 130, 245-9
Copa América 11
Costa Rica National Football Team 99-100
Costil, Benoît 90
Côte d'Ivoire National Football Team 167
Coupet, Grégory 71, 72, 78, 79, 92
Courtois, Thibaut 217
COVID-19 global pandemic 234-6
Crespo, Hernán 34
Cris 76, 82, 84
Croatia National Football Team 219-21
Crystal Palace FC 12, 178
Cudicini, Carlo 142

D

De Gea, David 187
De Zerbi, Jean-Marie 56, 62
Debbouze, Jamel 154
Delgado, Chelito 82-3
Demanget (HL's maternal great-grandfather), Cesar 35
Demanget (HL's maternal great-grandmother), Marthe 35
Dembélé, Ousmane 14, 206, 267, 269
Denmark National Football Team 209, 255
Depay, Memphis 204
Deschamps, Didier 4, 15, 116, 132, 133, 147-8, 153-4, 156, 166,

INDEX

204–5, 207–8, 212, 216, 219, 221, 240, 242, 261, 267
Diaby, Abou 48, 54
Diarra, Lassana 101, 131–2, 135–6
Dida 70
Dier, Eric 237
Digard, Didier 48, 54
Digne, Lucas 241
Djetou, Martin 224
Domenech, Raymond 89, 93, 94, 100, 102, 105–6, 107–8, 112, 129
Doyle, Kevin 96
Duverne, Robert 77, 112, 126
Dybala, Paulo 269, 270

E
Echouafni, Olivier 53, 67
Ecuador National Football Team 158
Eder 170–1
Elsner, Luka 55
Elsner, Rok 55
England National Football Team 129, 133, 162–3, 168, 258–61
English League Cup 198, 236
Escalettes, Jean-Pierre 114
Espírito Santo, Nuno 243–5
Estrosi, Christian 173
Europa League 140, 236, 237
European Championships, UEFA
 Euro Austria-Switzerland (2008) 89, 110
 Euro France (1984) 71
 Euro France (2016) 153, 157, 166–72, 218
 Euro Germany (2024) 18
 Euro multiple host countries (2020/2021) 12, 234, 239–43, 259
 Euro Poland-Ukraine (2012) 133–6, 148, 149
 Euro Portugal (2004) 172
 under-19s 54, 57, 58
Everton FC 151, 181, 236
Evra, Patrice 102, 107–8, 110, 112, 114, 116, 155, 171, 187
Eyjafjallajökull volcanic eruption 85–6

F
Fàbregas, Cesc 149
Faccioli, Marino 71, 75
fans 58, 189
Faroe Islands National Team 92–3
fatherhood 5, 13, 41, 121, 198, 199–200, 273–4, 280–1
Fellaini, Marouane 217
FIFA (Fédération Internationale de Football Association) 11, 222, 252–3, 266
 see also World Cup, FIFA
Fiorentina, AFC 35
Fofana, Youssouf 261
France 3 Provence-Alpes-Côte-d'Azur 58
France Football 10–11, 156
France National Football Team 9–10, 12–14, 21, 99, 41–2, 72, 99
 end-of-season tours 149–50
 Euro (2020/2021) 239–43
 Euro Austria-Switzerland (2008) 89
 Euro France (2016) 153, 157, 166–72, 218
 Euro Poland-Ukraine (2012) 133–4, 148, 149
 fallout from French World Cup strike (2010) 119–20
 HL's career with 9–10, 12–14, 21, 89–98, 99–117
 as captain 129–36, 147–50, 152–60, 161–72, 203–14, 217–22, 239–43, 251–71
 HL's favourite saves 213–14, 216–17
 HL's first call-up 89
 HL's first cap vs Uruguay (friendly) 90, 91
 HL's record caps for country 256, 258, 260, 261
 HL's retirement 14–19
 pre-World Cup (2022) politics and injuries 252–4
 pre-World Cup training camp, Tignes (2010) 100–1
 Stade de France–Paris terror attack (2015) 161–3
 under-15s and under-17s 45
 under-18s 47–8, 51, 91

INDEX

France National Football Team (*cont.*)
  under-19s 54, 57
  under-21s 62, 89, 90
  Valbuena-Benzema sex-tape scandal 163–6
  World Cup Brazil (2014) 157–60, 256
  World Cup France (1998) 224
  World Cup playoffs (1993) 153
  World Cup playoffs (2009 and 2010) 93–7, 150
  World Cup playoffs (2013) 148, 150, 152–6
  World Cup prep (2010) 101–2
  World Cup Qatar (2022) 1–6, 10–11, 23–4, 34, 251, 254–66
    final vs Argentina 18–19, 266–71
  World Cup qualifiers (2009) 92–3
  World Cup qualifiers (2012) 149
  World Cup qualifiers (2017) 204–5, 206
  World Cup Russia (2018) 6, 153, 156, 189, 208–19, 280–1
    final vs Croatia 219–22
  World Cup South Africa (2010) 87, 99–117
French Championship 71, 76, 79, 81, 87, 127
  under-18s 54–5, 58
French Cup (Coupe de France) 52, 127–8
French Football Federation (FFF) 102, 108, 109, 113, 114, 116, 120, 132, 147, 158, 225
French National Football Team Women's 91
Friedel, Brad 139, 140, 142
Fulham FC 22

G
Gace, Ismaël 55
Gallas, William 97, 102–3, 141
Galliani, Adriano 71
Garde, Rémi 71, 126, 130–1
Gasset, Jean-Louis 133m 187
Génésio, Bruno 77, 126
Geoffroy, Christophe 200
Germany National Football Team 90, 131, 132, 159–60, 161, 162, 168–9, 240
  under-18s 48
Gignac, André-Pierre 'Dédé' 105, 170
Ginola, David 53
Giroud, Olivier 4, 17, 141, 149, 153, 156, 168, 210, 223–4, 225–6, 254, 257, 259, 262, 263, 267, 269
Given, Shay 96
Godín, Diego 213–14
Golden Glove trophy 11
Gollini, Pierluigi 31, 247
Gomes, Heurelho 142
Gomis, Báfe 82
Gonalons, Max 82, 86
Gouffran, Yoan 54
Gourcuff, Yoann 48, 54, 71, 102, 110–11, 115, 120–1, 123, 125
Govou, Sidney 76, 82, 84
Grandfather (HL's paternal) 20, 33–4, 38, 40, 41, 61–2, 68
  influence on HL's football career 20, 41–3, 44, 45–6, 47, 60, 62, 275
Grandmother (HL's paternal) 2, 14–15, 19, 33–4, 38, 41, 45, 52, 62, 66, 69, 72, 95, 235, 255, 262, 277
Grange, Fabrice 92
Grégorini, Damien 51, 59
Grenier, Clément 153
Griezmann, Antoine 17, 162, 167–8, 169, 182, 209–10, 213, 217, 219, 254, 255, 258, 259, 262, 263, 269
Grosso, Fabio 76
Guardiola, Pep 192, 205–6, 237
Guedes, Frederico Chaves (Fred), 76, 79
Guerreiro, Raphaël 170, 171

H
Hardouin, Florence 116
Hasselbaink, Jimmy Floyd 53
Hazard, Eden 217
Henry, Thierry 91, 93, 97, 100–1, 107, 110, 113, 116
Herbette, Pascal 44
Hernández, Javier 'Chicharito' 215

INDEX

Hernández, Lucas 241, 254
Hernandez, Théo 254, 262
Higuaín, Gonzalo 83
Hitchen, Steve 237
Højbjerg, Pierre-Emile 237, 246
Honduras National Football Team 158
Hummels, Mats 160
Hungary National Football Team 241

I
Ibrahimović, Zlatan 134
Iceland National Football Team 167
Inter Milan, FC 63-4, 191
Israel National Football Team 153

J
Jennings, Pat 189
Jiménez, Toni 17, 144
Joly, Monsieur 40-1
Jourdren, Geoffrey 54, 91
Juninho 76, 79, 82
Juventus FC 190

K
Kaboul, Younès 48, 54, 141, 186
Kaká 83
Kalac, Željko 70-1
Källström, Kim 82
Kane, Harry 186, 193, 234, 237, 244, 246, 259-60, 261
Kanté, N'Golo 3-4, 210, 222, 253
Kolo Muani, Randal 262, 267, 269, 270
Koné, Baky 175-6
Koscielny, Laurent 'Lolo' 141, 152, 153, 171, 206, 223-6
Kulusevski, Dejan 247

L
Lacombe, Bernard 75, 123-4
Laigle, Pierre 224
Lama, Bernard 71-2
Lamatina, Fabien 55
Lamela, Coco 230, 236
Lamouchi, Sabri 53, 224
Laporte, Aymeric 238
Larbi, Kamel 53, 54, 55
Laslandes, Lilian 67, 78

Lazio, SS 26, 64, 140
Le Graët, Noël 108, 110, 116, 147, 154, 264
Le Havre, AC 55, 276
League Cup, French 57, 276
    Final (2006) 57-8, 59
    HL's professional debut (2005) 56
Leicester City FC 187, 188, 191, 257
Leipzig, RB 234
Lemar, Thomas 206
Lens, RC 63
Lenval Children's Hospital, Nice 256-7
L'Équipe 10, 14, 16-17, 95, 107, 225
Letizi, Lionel 60-1, 224
Levy, Daniel 16, 24, 25, 26, 137, 138, 144, 189-90, 196, 237-8, 244, 275
Lewandowski, Robert 257
Ligue 1, French 52-3, 55, 57, 60-4, 79, 87
    see also French Championship;
        French Cup; Olympique
        Gymnaste Club de Nice;
        Olympique Lyonnais;
        individual clubs by name
Ligue 2, French 55
Ligue Méditerranée 41-2, 44, 91
Lille, LOSC 67-8
Liverpool FC 82, 190, 193, 194-6
Llorente, Fernando 192, 194
Lloris (HL's daughter), Anna-Rose 13, 73, 121, 139, 140, 141, 218, 219, 222, 255, 264, 273-4, 281
Lloris (née Demanget - HL's mother), Christine 35, 37, 38-40, 65, 275
Lloris (HL's brother), Gautier 33, 36, 38, 39-40, 55, 66, 69, 70, 72, 119, 162, 218, 260, 276-7
Lloris (HL's daughter), Giuliana 158, 218, 219, 222, 255, 264, 273-4, 281
Lloris, Hugo
    angry outbursts 180-3
    argument with Son Heung-min 181-2
    arrest for drunk driving 226-31
    Ballon d'Or nominations 277

INDEX

Lloris, Hugo (*cont.*)
   beach soccer tournament 53
   brother's football career 276-7
   career memorabilia 277-8
   Cedac de Cimiez 20, 36-7, 42, 178
   childhood/family background 19-20, 33-42, 178
   COVID-19 pandemic 234-6
   family skiing holiday 178
   fatherhood 5, 13, 41, 121, 198, 199-200, 273-4, 280-1
   financial investments 278-9
   football and life in LA 273-4
   future in football 279-80
   goalie craziness 175, 177-8, 180-2
   grandfather's death 61-2
   grandfather's influence on football career 20, 41-3, 44, 45-6, 47, 62, 275
   Ibiza quad bike accident 178-9
   inspirational footballers 34-5, 59, 83, 278
   on knocking Baky Koné unconscious 175-6
   leaving Spurs 23-32, 274
   Ligue Méditerranée 41-2
   mental health 23-4
   mother's death 65-70, 276
   as patron of the Lenval Foundation 256-7
   physical health/injuries 13, 22-3, 64, 80-1, 82, 150-2, 178-9, 198-200, 215-16
   post-World Cup win anti-doping test 222, 225
   professional debut 56
   risk taking 178-80
   rivalry with other French goalies 89, 90-2, 94
   school education 40-1, 46, 47, 48-9, 51, 275
   tennis 36, 43
   terror attacks in Nice (2016) 172-3
   terror attacks in Paris (2015) 161-3
   top five saves 214-17
   transfer discussions/opportunities 64-5, 70-2

   UEFA under-19s Championship (2005) 54
   Valbuena-Benzema sex-tape scandal 163-6
   World Cup Final Qatar (2022) 266-71
   World Cup Final Russia (2018) 219-22, 280-1
   see also France National Football Team; Olympique Gymnaste Club de Nice; Olympique Lyonnais; Tottenham Hotspur FC

Lloris (HL's son), Léandro 198, 264, 273-4
Lloris (HL's father), Luc 2, 14-15, 34, 35, 37, 38-9, 41, 44, 46-7, 48, 49, 66, 68, 69, 71, 72, 75, 117, 119, 218, 255, 275, 276
Lloris (HL's wife), Marine 2, 41, 49, 57, 66, 70, 72-3, 119, 137, 140, 141, 158, 192, 218, 227, 235, 255, 273-4
Lloris (HL's sister), Sabrina 7, 33, 35, 37-8, 40, 70, 218, 275
Lo Celso, Giovani 236
Lollichon, Christophe 144-5
López, Claudio 34
López, Lisandro 'Licha' 82, 83-5, 125, 131, 139, 230
Lorient, FC 55
Los Angeles FC 273-4
Lotito, Claudio 26, 64
Lovren, Dejan 194-5
Lukaku, Romelu 150, 217
Luxembourg National Football Team 206

M
Macron, Emmanuel 4
Maignan, Mike 18
Makoun, Jean II 83
Malouda, Flo 132
Manchester City FC 22, 190, 191-2, 206, 234, 236, 238, 244
Manchester United FC 179, 187, 227-8, 229, 245, 246

INDEX

Mandanda, Steve 89–90, 91, 92, 94, 221, 255–6, 258
Mandžukić, Mario 219, 220
Maradona, Diego 159
Marange, Florian 54
March for Equality and Against Racism (1983) 154
The Marchers film (2013) 154
Marciniak, Szymon 266, 270
Margotton, Grégoire 216
Marseille, Olympique de *see* Olympique de Marseille
Martel, Gervais 63
Martínez, Emiliano 10–11, 268–9, 270
Martínez, Lautaro 269
Martini, Bruno 92, 96
Mascherano, Javier 210
Mason, Ryan 237, 249
Matuidi, Blaise 3–4, 156, 169, 207, 208, 263
Mbappé, Kylian 17, 206, 209, 219, 220, 222, 242, 254, 257, 258, 260, 263, 264, 268, 269
media/press 10–11, 14, 19, 58, 95, 102, 109, 111, 113–14, 119, 132–4, 163, 164, 166, 227, 229, 252, 260–1
Ménez, Jérémy 136
mental health 23–4
Messi, Lionel 209, 210–11, 266, 268, 269–70
Messina, Cédric 35
Messina, Danielle 35
Messina, David 35
Messina, Marcel 35
Messina, Warren 35
Mexès, Philippe 132
Mexico National Football Team 104–7
Milan, AC 70–1, 72
Monaco, AS 58, 123, 150
Montiel, Gonzalo 270–1
Morocco 34
Morocco National Football Team 34, 261–2
Moura, Lucas 193, 194
Mourinho, José 6, 126–7, 182, 201, 233–4, 235–9, 278
Moutaouakil, Yassin 54

Muñoz, Hilaire 51, 52
Mura, NŠ 247
Muslera, Fernando 104, 213

N
Nancy Lorraine, AS 57–8
Nantes, FC 61
Nasri, Samir 132, 133–6, 153–4
Nations League, UEFA 12–13
Netherlands National Football Team 204, 269
Neuer, Manuel 54, 159–60, 168
Newcastle United FC 23, 151
N'Gog, David 216
Niang, Mamadou 63
Nice city 57–8, 173–4
Nice-Matin 42, 45
Nice, OGC
  see Olympique Gymnaste Club de Nice
Nigeria National Football Team 159
Nkunku, Christopher 253
Northern Ireland National Team 189
Norwich City FC 146, 234

O
Olić, Ivica 86–7
Olympique de Marseille 41, 63, 90, 93–4, 150, 175–6
Olympique Gymnaste Club de Nice 39, 42–6, 47, 122, 124, 130, 180
  B team 51, 52, 58
  Brigade Sud ultras 58
  HL's favourite save 215–16
  HL's Ligue 1 pro career 51–3, 60–4, 65, 66–8, 69
  League Cup Final (2006) 57–8, 59
  under-18s teams 42–6, 47, 51, 52, 55–6, 58
Olympique Lyonnais 16, 55, 60, 64, 69, 89, 120–1, 125, 130–1, 143, 165, 276
  Champions League (2007-2008) 80
  Champions League (2008-2009) 82
  Champions League (2009-2010) 81, 83–4, 85–7, 99, 215
  Champions League (2011-2012) 126
  Coupe de France (2011-2012) 127–8

289

INDEX

Olympique Lyonnais (*cont.*)
    derbies against AS Saint-Étienne 78-9, 121
    French Championship 71, 76, 79, 81, 82, 87, 127-8
    HL knocks Baky Koné unconscious 175-6
    HL leaves 137-9
    HL's 2010-2011 season 121-2, 125
    HL's 2011-2012 season 126-7
    HL's favourite save 215
    HL's Nice stadium tunnel outburst caught on camera 180
    HL's professional career with 71-2, 75-87, 93-8, 120-8, 130-1
    Trophée des Champions 79, 128

P
Padovani, Franck 54, 55
paparazzi 227, 229
Paratici, Fabio 31, 247
Paredes, Leandro 270
Paris Saint-Germain (PSG) FC 42, 53, 63, 72, 128, 186, 187, 216
Parks, Tony 143
Patrício, Rui 169
Pavard, Benjamin 210, 265
Payet, Dimitri 121, 166, 167
Pecastaing, Mathieu 55
Perišić, Ivan 219
Perret, Patrick 82
Perrin, Alain 79
Peru National Football Team 208
physical health/injuries 13, 22-3, 64, 80-1, 82, 150-2, 178-9, 198-9, 215-16
Pionetti, Enrico 51
Pjanic, Miré 83
Pochettino, Mauricio 6, 17-18, 143, 144, 179, 193, 194, 197, 200-1, 229
Pogba, Paul 156, 167, 210, 218, 219, 220, 242, 253, 263
Poland National Football Team 257
Ponsot, Vincent 124-5, 138
Portugal National Football Team 167, 169-72, 219, 240, 261

Postecoglou, Ange 27
Pouplin, Simon 144-5
Premier League football, UK 22, 145-6, 179, 190, 234-5, 238, 245
    see also individual teams by name; Tottenham Hotspur FC
Provedel, Ivan 26
PSV Eindhoven 83, 191
Puel, Claude 75, 77, 122, 125-6, 130

Q
Quevilly-Rouen Métropole, US 127-8

R
Rabiot, Adrien 241, 254, 266
Racing Club de Avellaneda 85
rainbow armbands and LGBT+ issues 252-3
Rami, Adil 211-12
Ramos, Juande 70, 83
Raviot, Franck 6, 15, 189, 221, 256, 269
Real Madrid CF 83-4, 126-7, 169, 187, 278
Rebić, Ante 220
Redissi, Abdel 82
Regragui, Walid 262
Rémy, Loïc 153
Rennes FC, Stade 180
Republic of Ireland National Football Team 93, 94, 95-6, 150, 167, 168, 278
Réveillére, Anthony 76, 82
Ribéry, Franck 86, 105, 106, 110-11, 120, 157
Richarlison 247
Ricort, Roger 51
Riou, Rémy 90
Robben, Arjen 86
Rodriguez, Ricardo 241
Rohr, Gernot 53
Romania National Football Team 93, 166, 167
Romero, Cristian 266-7
Ronaldo (Brazilian) 176
Ronaldo, Cristiano 83, 169, 172, 177, 246
Rool, Cyril 67

INDEX

Rosalinde Rancher primary school 40–1
Rothen, Jérôme 216
Russian National Football Team 163

S
Sagna, Bacary 141
Saint-Étienne, AS 41, 78, 121
Sakho, Mamadou 153, 155, 156
Sammaritano, Frédéric 54
school education 40–1, 46, 47, 48–9, 51, 275
Sedan Ardennes, CS 63
Serbia National Football Team 93
Sheffield United FC 181
Sherwood, Tim 144
Shevchenko, Andriy 134
Sidibé, Djibril 207
Sissoko, Moussa 169, 194, 195
Skomina, Damir 195
Son Heung-min 181–2, 191, 234
South Africa National Football Team 115–16
Sow, Moussa 54
Spain National Football Team 99, 133, 134–5, 149, 243
Spinosi, Laurent 176
Squillaci, Sébastien 141
Stellini, Cristian 22, 249
Stéphan, Guy 218–19
Sterling, Raheem 192
the *Sun* 227
Sweden National Football Team 89, 134, 204–5, 206
Switzerland National Football Team 12, 158, 239, 241–3

T
Tchouaméni, Aurélien 11, 254, 270
Téléfoot TV show 111, 226
Tennis Club des Combes, Nice 36
terror attacks (2016), Promenade des Anglais, Nice 172–3
terror attacks (2015), Stade de France/Paris 161–3
TF1 television channel 14, 19
Thuram, Lilian 12–13, 257, 258, 260
Thuram, Marcus 267
Tigres UANL 170
Toivonen, Ola 204
Toldo, Francesco 35
Tolisso, Corentin 217
Tottenham Hotspur FC 6–7, 9–10, 11–12, 70, 72, 125, 130, 163
 Amazon documentary 181, 182, 197–8, 201, 238–9
 Antonio Conte's management 245–9
 career with 137–46, 150–2, 179–82, 185–201, 205, 227–8, 229, 233–49
 Champions League 187–8, 190–4, 198, 215, 234
  final vs Liverpool (2019) 194–7
 Europa League 140, 236, 237
 HL fractures elbow 198–200
 HL leaves 21–32, 274
 HL sidelined by André Villas-Boas 139–44
 HL's argument with teammate Son Heung-min 181–2
 HL's contract offer 85
 HL's early talks with 70, 72
 HL's favourite save 214–15
 HL's head injury 150–2
 HL's transfer to 137–8
 impact of COVID-19 234–6
 José Mourinho's management 201, 233–4, 235–9
 League Cup 195, 198, 236
 Mauricio Pochettino's management 185–201, 229, 234
 Nuno Espírito Santo's management 243–5
 Premier League Final (2021) 238
 rumours of HL's outward transfers 186–7
 White Hart Lane stadium 145, 187–8
Toulalan, Jérémy 76, 82, 86, 109, 119
Toulon, SC 55
Toulon Tournament 62
Toulouse FC 180
Tout le sport TV show 58
Trapattoni, Giovanni 95, 96
Trophée des Champions 79, 128

INDEX

Tunisia National Football Team 90, 101-2, 255
Turkey National Football Team 92

U
Ukraine National Football Team 134, 148, 150, 152-3, 155-6
Umtiti, Samuel 171, 217, 220
Union of European Football Association (UEFA)
  Conference League 246
  Cup Championship 58
  Nations League 12-13
  under-19s Championship (2005) 54, 57
  see also Champions League
United Sates of America National Football Team 207
Upamecano, Dayot 254
Uruguay National Football Team 90-1, 104, 147, 211, 212-13

V
Valbuena-Benzema sex-tape scandal 163-6
Valbuena, Mathieu 153, 163-5
Valencia CF 34-5
Valenciennes FC 63, 138
Valencony, Bruno 51, 52, 53, 56-7
Varane, Raphaël 4, 17, 153, 213, 219, 220, 253, 262-3
Vardy, Jamie 178, 191
Ventrone, Gian Piero 248

Vercoutre, Rémy 78, 84
Veschi, Didier 47
Vialli, Gianluca 249
Vicario, Guglielmo 24, 29-30
Vieira, Patrick 12, 91, 110
Villa-Boas, André 138, 139, 140, 141-3, 151

W
Wathelet, Alain 39
Wenger, Arsène 137
West Ham FC 166
White Hart Lane stadium 145, 187-8
World Cup, FIFA
  Brazil (2014) 157-60, 256
  France (1998) 177, 224
  Germany (2006) 16
  Mexico (1986) 98
  Qatar (2022) 1-6, 10-11, 18-19, 23-4, 34, 251, 254-71
  Russia (2018) 6, 153, 156, 189, 208-14, 217-22, 259, 280-1
  South Africa (2010) 87, 99-117, 213
  Spain (1982) 189
  USA (1994) 153
  USA, Canada and Mexico (2026) 280

Z
Zahia sex scandal 102
Zenden, Boudewijn 176
Zidane, Zinedine 132
Žigić, Nikola 93

TRANSLATOR'S THANKS

I would like to thank Les Bleus superfan Olivier Raynal – with whom I shared the passion and excitement of watching both of France's World Cup victories together in 1998 and 2018 – my colleague Paul Russell Garrett for a crucial tip and editor Ian Preece who did a sterling job, for which I am most grateful.